## C.E.L. WELSH

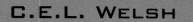

# HARRY HOUDINI

## CAMPFIRE™

### KALYANI NAVYUG MEDIA PVT LTD
New Delhi

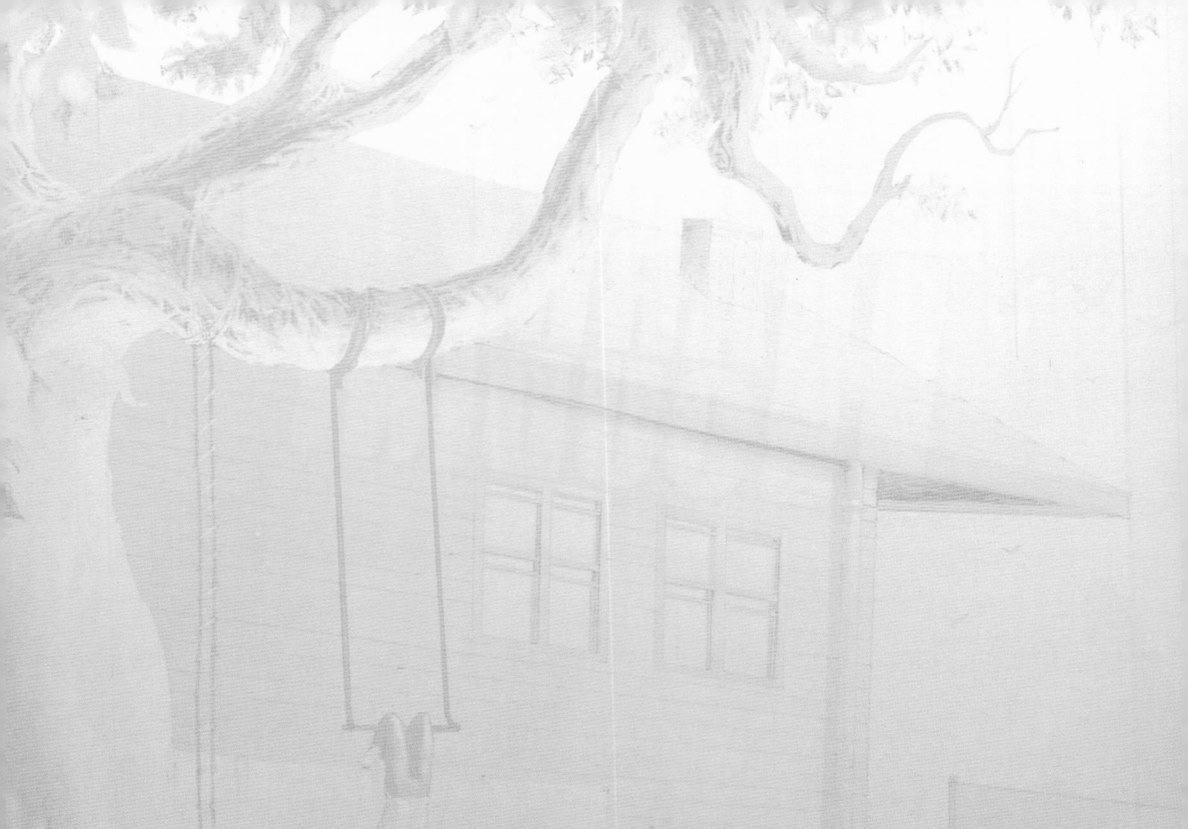

Sitting around the Campfire, telling the story, were:

| | | |
|---|---|---|
| **Author** | : | C.E.L. Welsh |
| **Illustrator** | : | Lalit Kumar Singh |
| **Illustrations Editor** | : | Jayshree Das |
| **Colorist** | : | Rajiv Chauhan |
| **Color Consultant** | : | R.C. Prakash |
| **Letterers** | : | Vishal Sharma |
| | | Bhavnath Chaudhary |
| **Editors** | : | Suparna Deb |
| | | Mark Jones |
| **Research Editor** | : | Pushpanjali Borooah |

**Cover Artists:**

| | | |
|---|---|---|
| **Illustrator** | : | Lalit Kumar Singh |
| **Colorist** | : | R.C. Prakash |
| **Designer** | : | Manishi Gupta |

Published by Kalyani Navyug Media Pvt Ltd
101 C, Shiv House, Hari Nagar Ashram
New Delhi 110014
India
www.campfire.co.in

ISBN: 978-93-80028-25-5

Printed in India at Tara Art Printers Pvt Ltd.

## About the Author

Christopher Welsh is an American freelance writer who owes comic books a great deal. He first read one over his brother's shoulder, feeling thrilled as Spider-man battled super villains and struggled with maintaining a secret identity. Through comics he learned a great deal about heroism, literature, storytelling and writing. When graphic novels—huge comic books with deep and satisfying stories—came along in the 1980s, he fell in love with them.

Like many others, Christopher's first introduction to fantasy fiction came from C.S. Lewis's *The Chronicles of Narnia,* soon followed by J.R.R. Tolkien's *The Lord of the Rings.* It was after reading these that Christopher knew he would be an author some day, and he began to pen short stories of all kinds.

In 2005, Christopher left his 'real' job to become a full-time writer, utilizing the Internet to find clients in Russia, England, Germany and Canada. When the opportunity came along to write graphic novels for Campfire, India was added to the list.

Christopher has worked all over the world, without leaving his home in Orlando, Florida. There he lives with his lovely wife, two wonderful children, and a dog named Iroh. He is currently working on his first novel and, of course, his next graphic novel from Campfire.

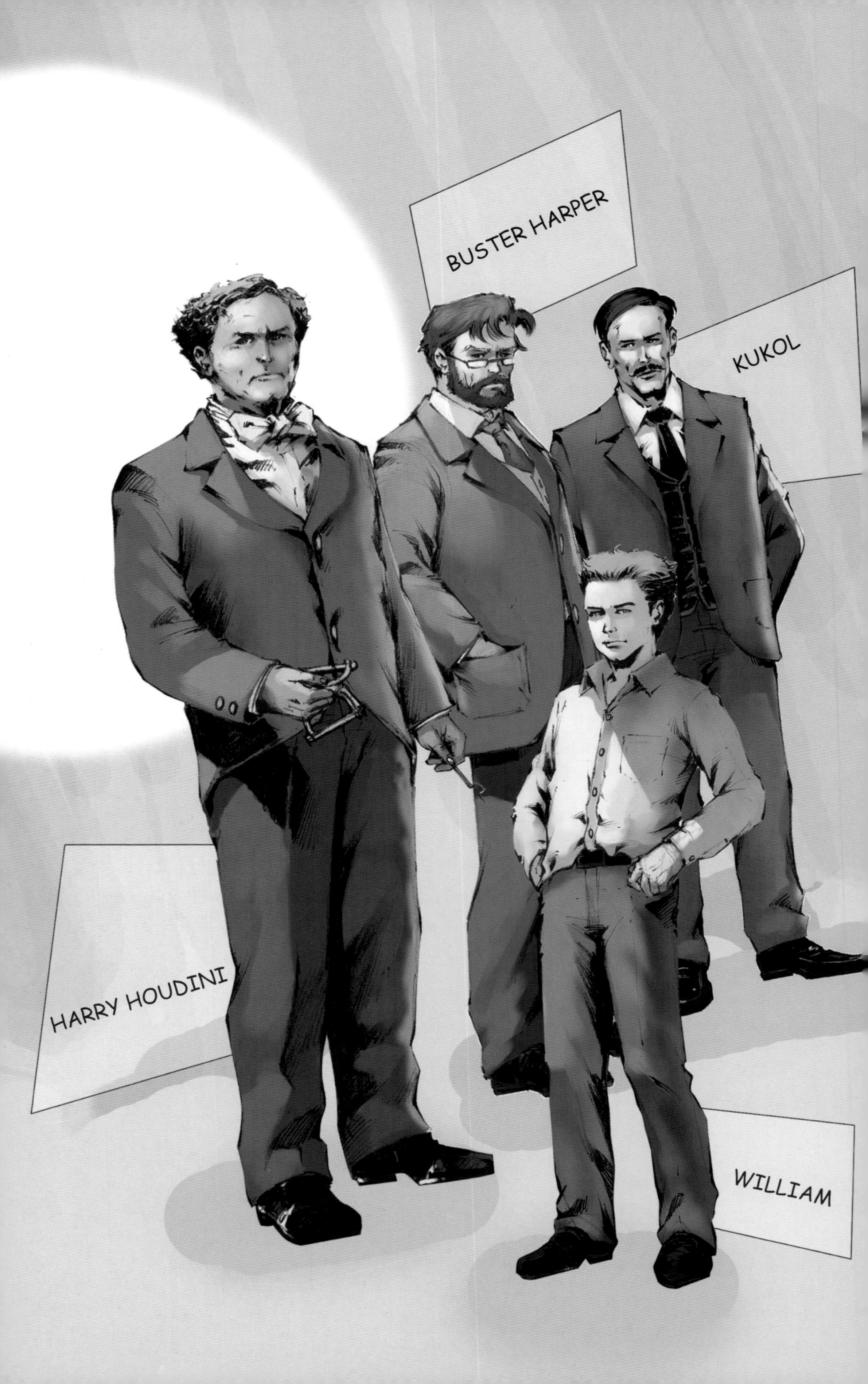
BUSTER HARPER
KUKOL
HARRY HOUDINI
WILLIAM

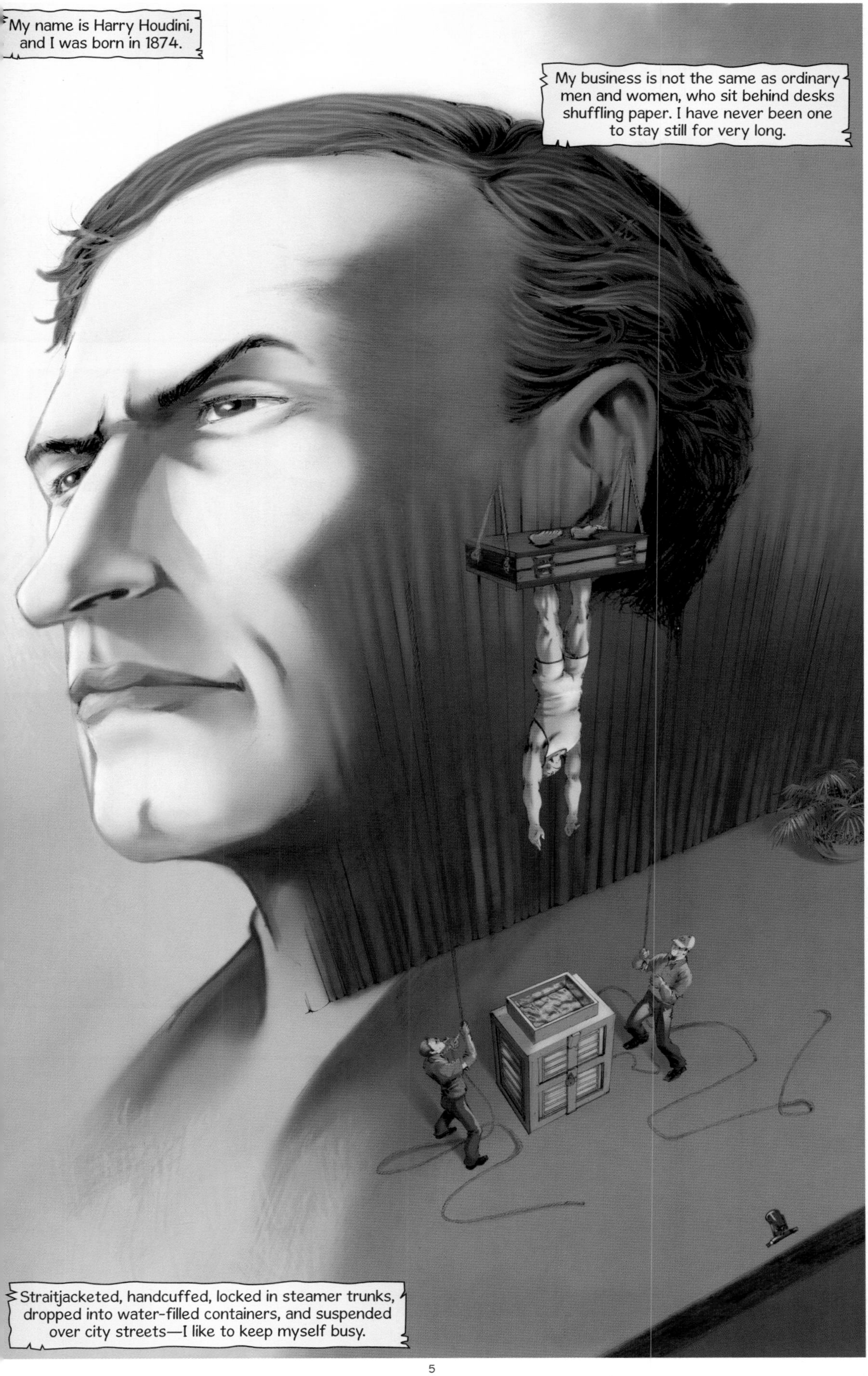
My name is Harry Houdini, and I was born in 1874.
My business is not the same as ordinary men and women, who sit behind desks shuffling paper. I have never been one to stay still for very long.
Straitjacketed, handcuffed, locked in steamer trunks, dropped into water-filled containers, and suspended over city streets—I like to keep myself busy.

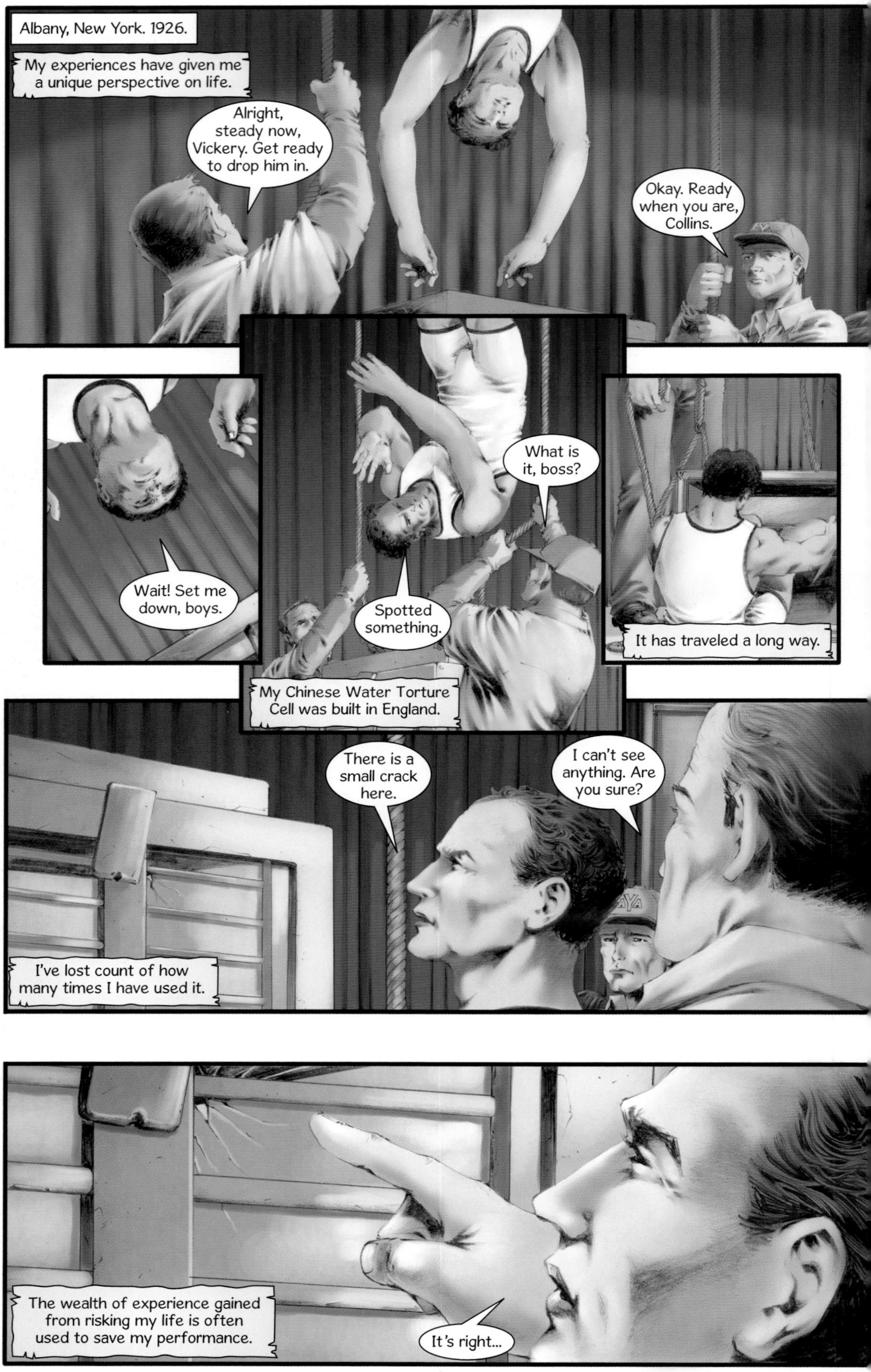
Albany, New York. 1926.
My experiences have given me a unique perspective on life.
Alright, steady now, Vickery. Get ready to drop him in.
Okay. Ready when you are, Collins.
Wait! Set me down, boys.
What is it, boss?
Spotted something.
My Chinese Water Torture Cell was built in England.
It has traveled a long way.
There is a small crack here.
I can't see anything. Are you sure?
I've lost count of how many times I have used it.
The wealth of experience gained from risking my life is often used to save my performance.
It's right...

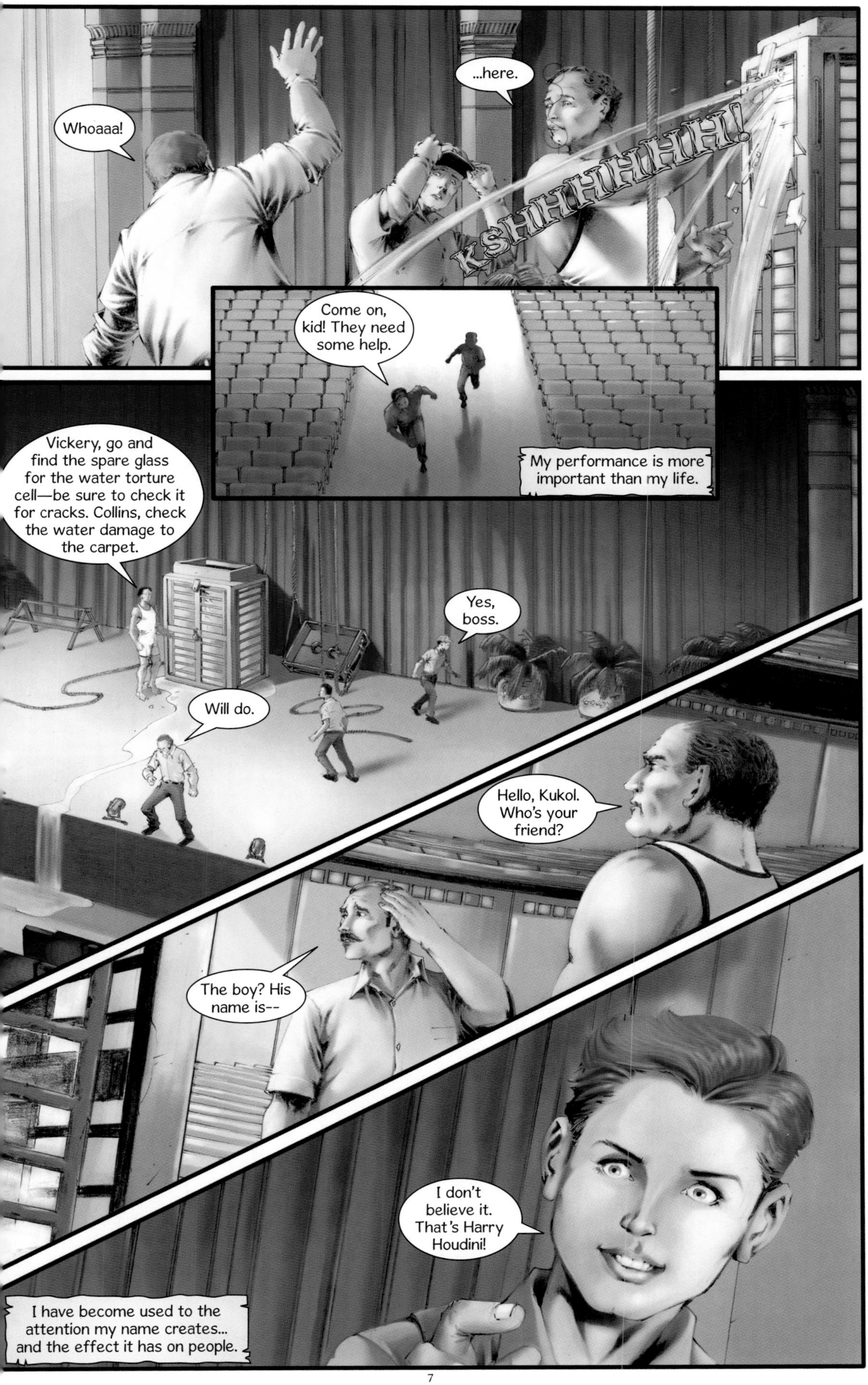
Whoaaa!
...here.
KSHHHHHHH!
Come on, kid! They need some help.
My performance is more important than my life.
Vickery, go and find the spare glass for the water torture cell—be sure to check it for cracks. Collins, check the water damage to the carpet.
Yes, boss.
Will do.
Hello, Kukol. Who's your friend?
The boy? His name is--
I don't believe it. That's Harry Houdini!
I have become used to the attention my name creates... and the effect it has on people.

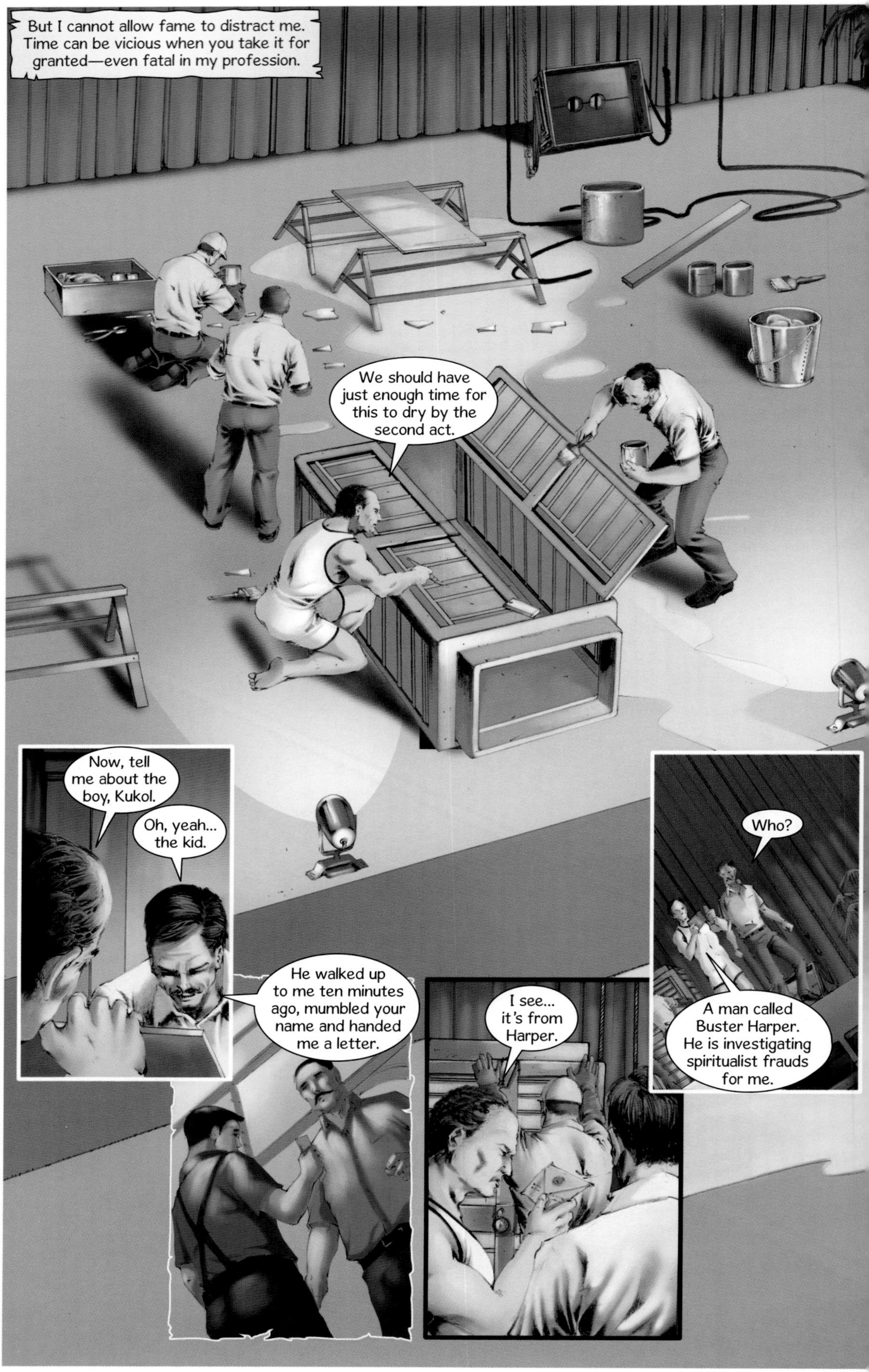

But I cannot allow fame to distract me. Time can be vicious when you take it for granted—even fatal in my profession.
We should have just enough time for this to dry by the second act.
Now, tell me about the boy, Kukol.
Oh, yeah... the kid.
He walked up to me ten minutes ago, mumbled your name and handed me a letter.
I see... it's from Harper.
Who?
A man called Buster Harper. He is investigating spiritualist frauds for me.

*The Journal of Doctor Buster Harper*

*September 15, 1926*

Here begins my first attempt at writing a journal. I have received a letter from Harry Houdini today. It seems the number of negative reports made about him by members of the spiritualist movement are increasing. Ever since he appeared before Congress to debunk the lot of them, their general attitude towards him has become hostile.

Even Houdini's former friend, Sir Arthur Conan Doyle, has now become his enemy.

*October 1, 1926*

Houdini told me I only had to ask if I needed a favor from him. Recently, it has occurred to me that there is one way in which he could help me. It has now been a year since my poor sister passed away, and her son, William, has been lost without her and somewhat directionless.

However, it seems William has developed an interest in magic, although he hasn't even fanned a deck of cards or made a coin disappear yet. But with the right guidance...

I will write at once to Houdini and ask if he will allow my nephew to work for him.

October 10, 1926
My nephew, William, has now
departed. He should arrive in
Albany tomorrow, and he will be
carrying a letter of introduction
from me.

I hope that my friend, Houdini, can help him out of his
depression and teach him a thing or two about magic.


October 11, 1926
Due to my close working proximity to Houdini, I have
decided to write a book about him. I will seek his
permission to do so, but I sense he would be more than
happy to have an account of his life. Obviously, it must
contain the truth, and not be made up like a lot of
newspaper articles that are appearing at the moment.

I shall first try to decide on a title for the book: The Master
Mystifier? The Elusive Artist? Or perhaps The Self Liberator?

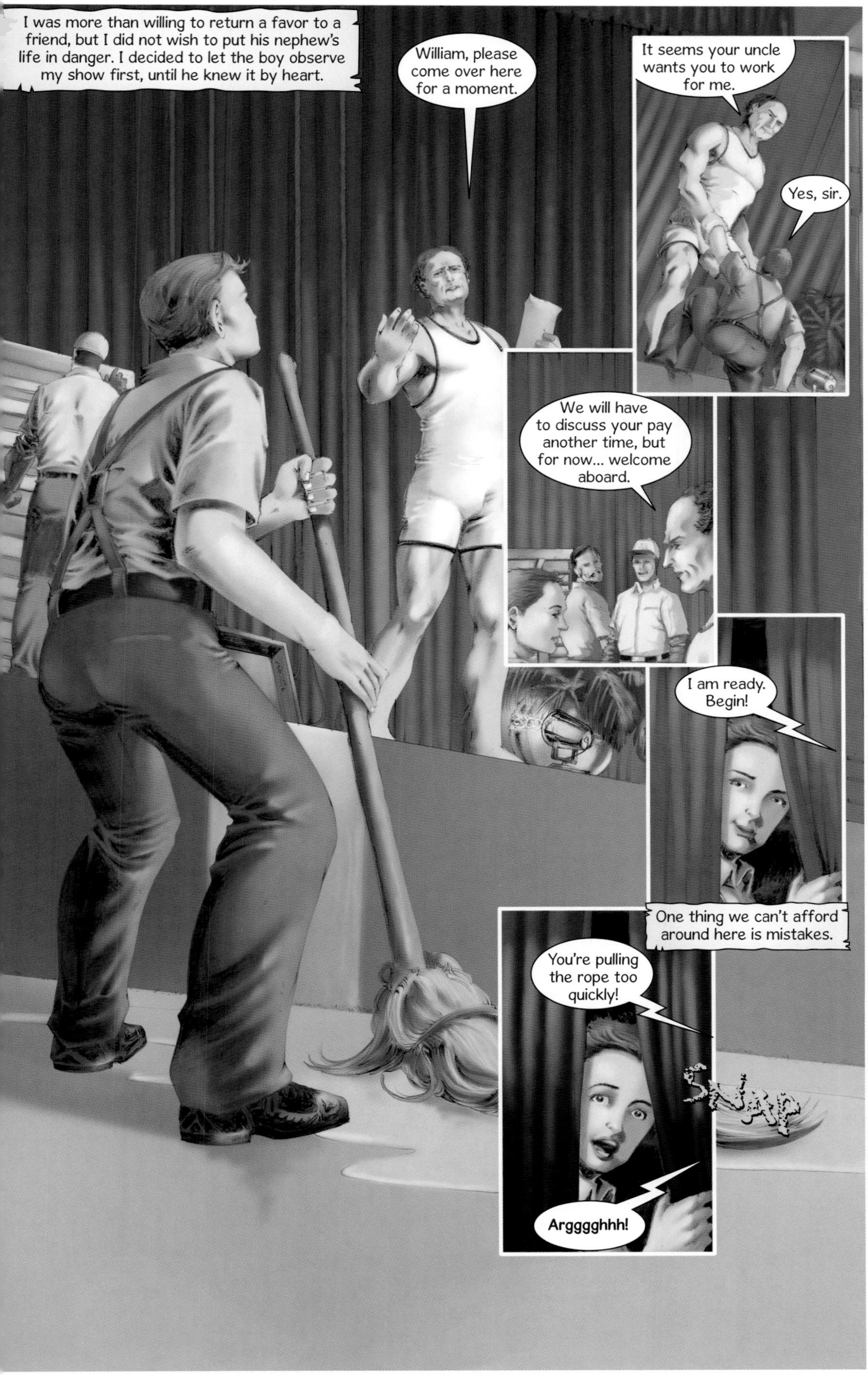
I was more than willing to return a favor to a friend, but I did not wish to put his nephew's life in danger. I decided to let the boy observe my show first, until he knew it by heart.
William, please come over here for a moment.
It seems your uncle wants you to work for me.
Yes, sir.
We will have to discuss your pay another time, but for now... welcome aboard.
I am ready. Begin!
One thing we can't afford around here is mistakes.
You're pulling the rope too quickly!
Argggghhh!

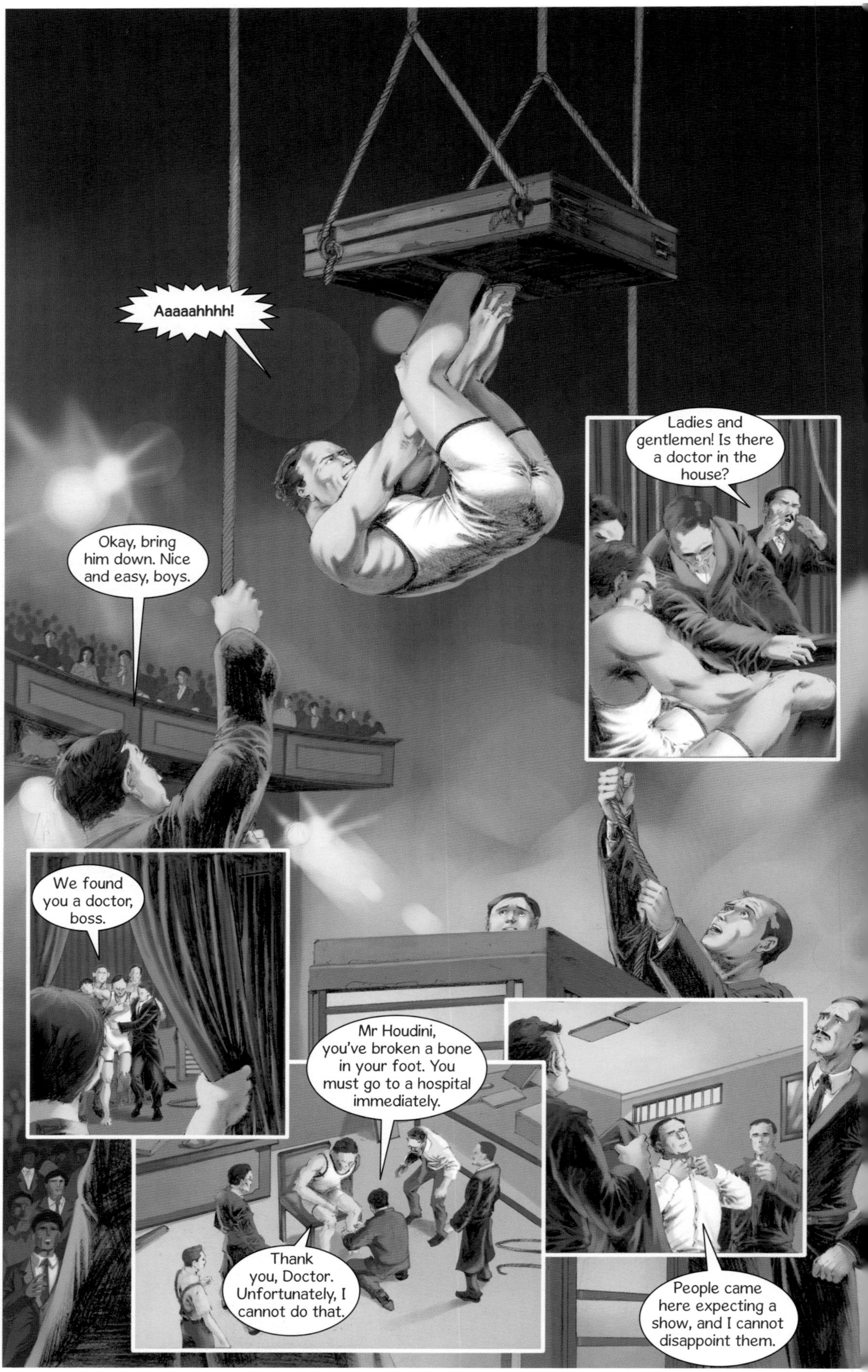
Aaaaahhhh!
Okay, bring him down. Nice and easy, boys.
Ladies and gentlemen! Is there a doctor in the house?
We found you a doctor, boss.
Mr Houdini, you've broken a bone in your foot. You must go to a hospital immediately.
Thank you, Doctor. Unfortunately, I cannot do that.
People came here expecting a show, and I cannot disappoint them.

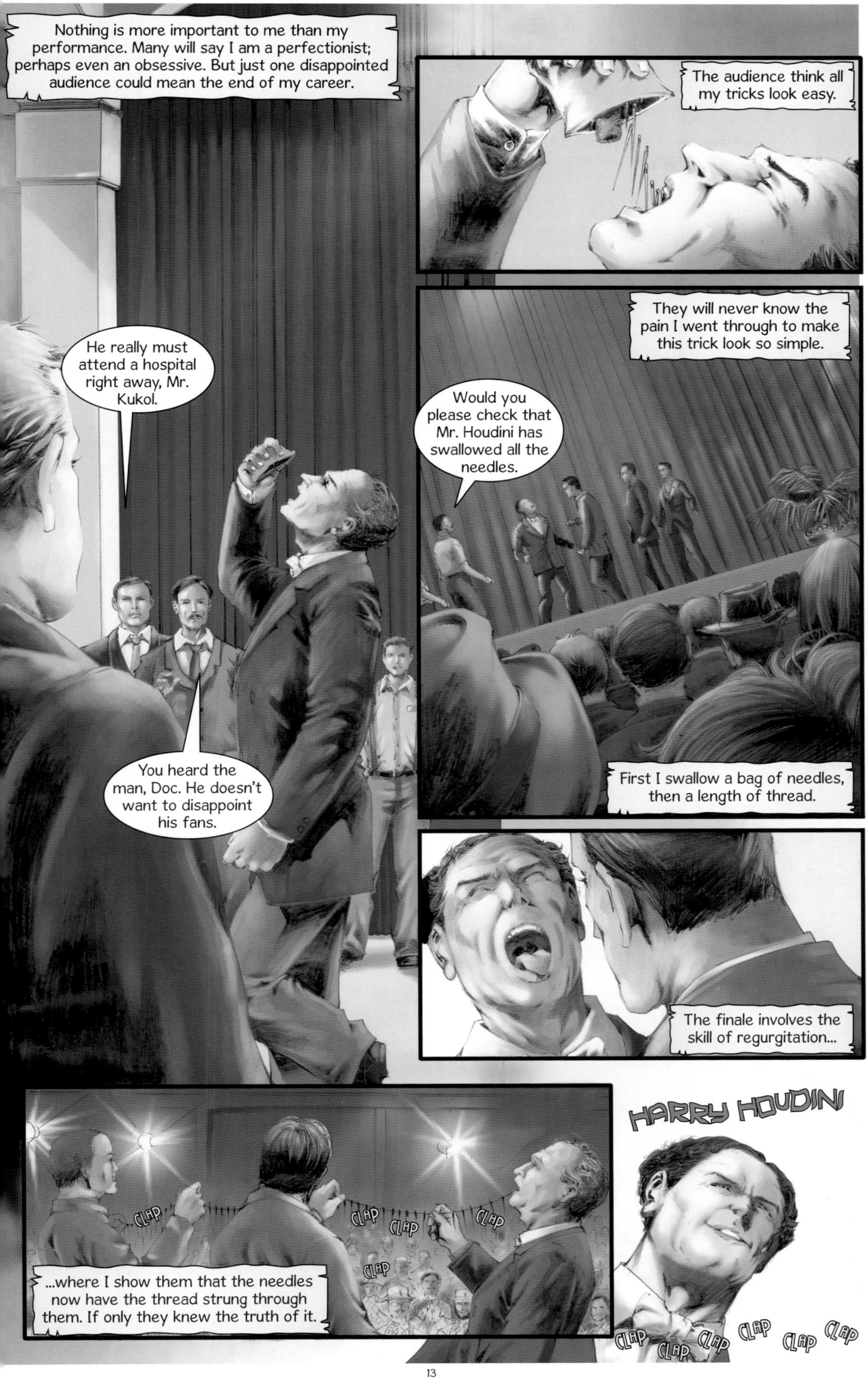
Nothing is more important to me than my performance. Many will say I am a perfectionist; perhaps even an obsessive. But just one disappointed audience could mean the end of my career.
The audience think all my tricks look easy.
He really must attend a hospital right away, Mr. Kukol.
You heard the man, Doc. He doesn't want to disappoint his fans.
They will never know the pain I went through to make this trick look so simple.
Would you please check that Mr. Houdini has swallowed all the needles.
First I swallow a bag of needles, then a length of thread.
The finale involves the skill of regurgitation...
...where I show them that the needles now have the thread strung through them. If only they knew the truth of it.
CLAP
CLAP
CLAP
CLAP
CLAP
HARRY HOUDINI
CLAP CLAP CLAP CLAP CLAP CLAP

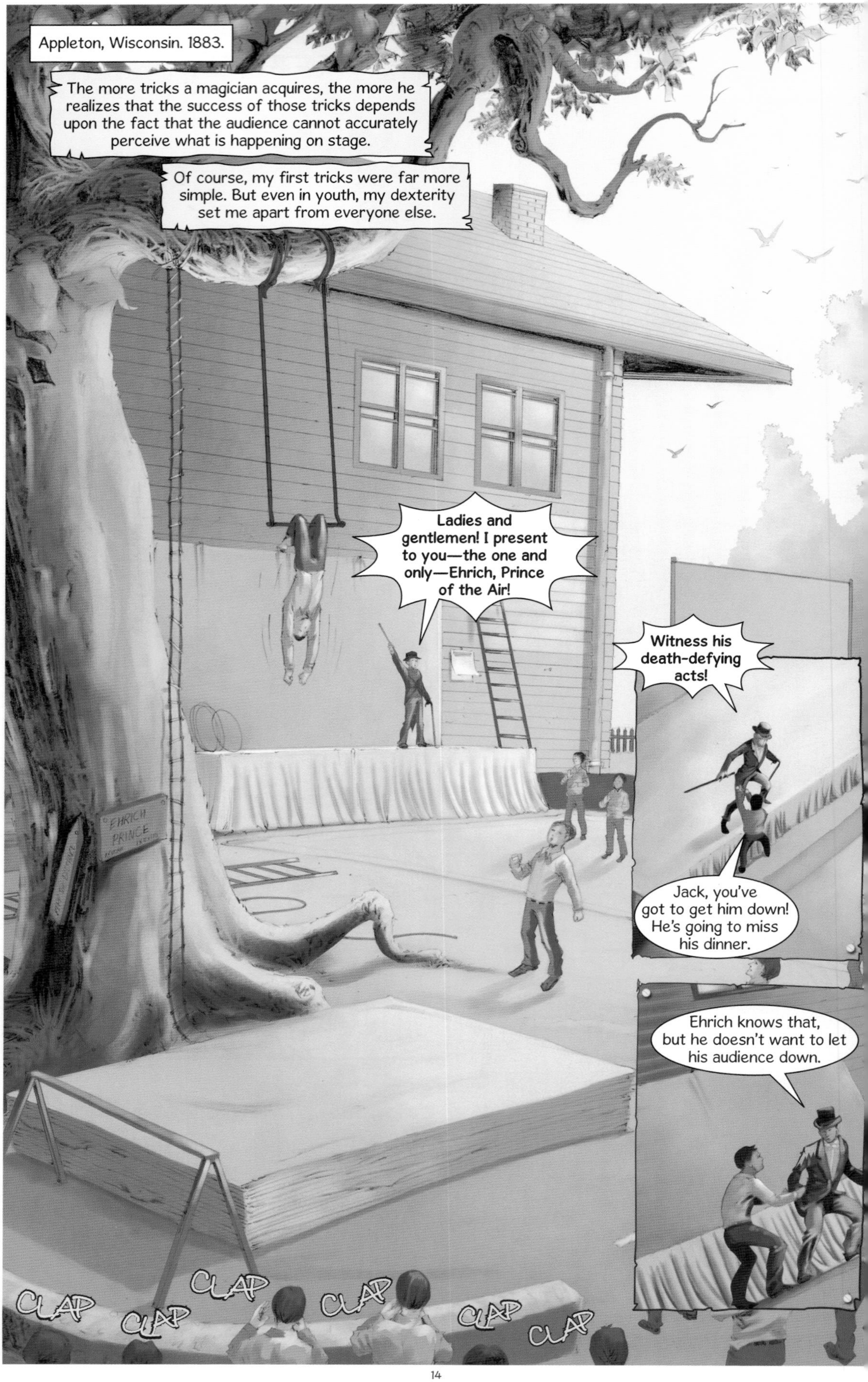
Appleton, Wisconsin. 1883.
The more tricks a magician acquires, the more he realizes that the success of those tricks depends upon the fact that the audience cannot accurately perceive what is happening on stage.
Of course, my first tricks were far more simple. But even in youth, my dexterity set me apart from everyone else.
Ladies and gentlemen! I present to you—the one and only—Ehrich, Prince of the Air!
EHRICH PRINCE
Witness his death-defying acts!
Jack, you've got to get him down! He's going to miss his dinner.
Ehrich knows that, but he doesn't want to let his audience down.
CLAP CLAP CLAP CLAP CLAP CLAP

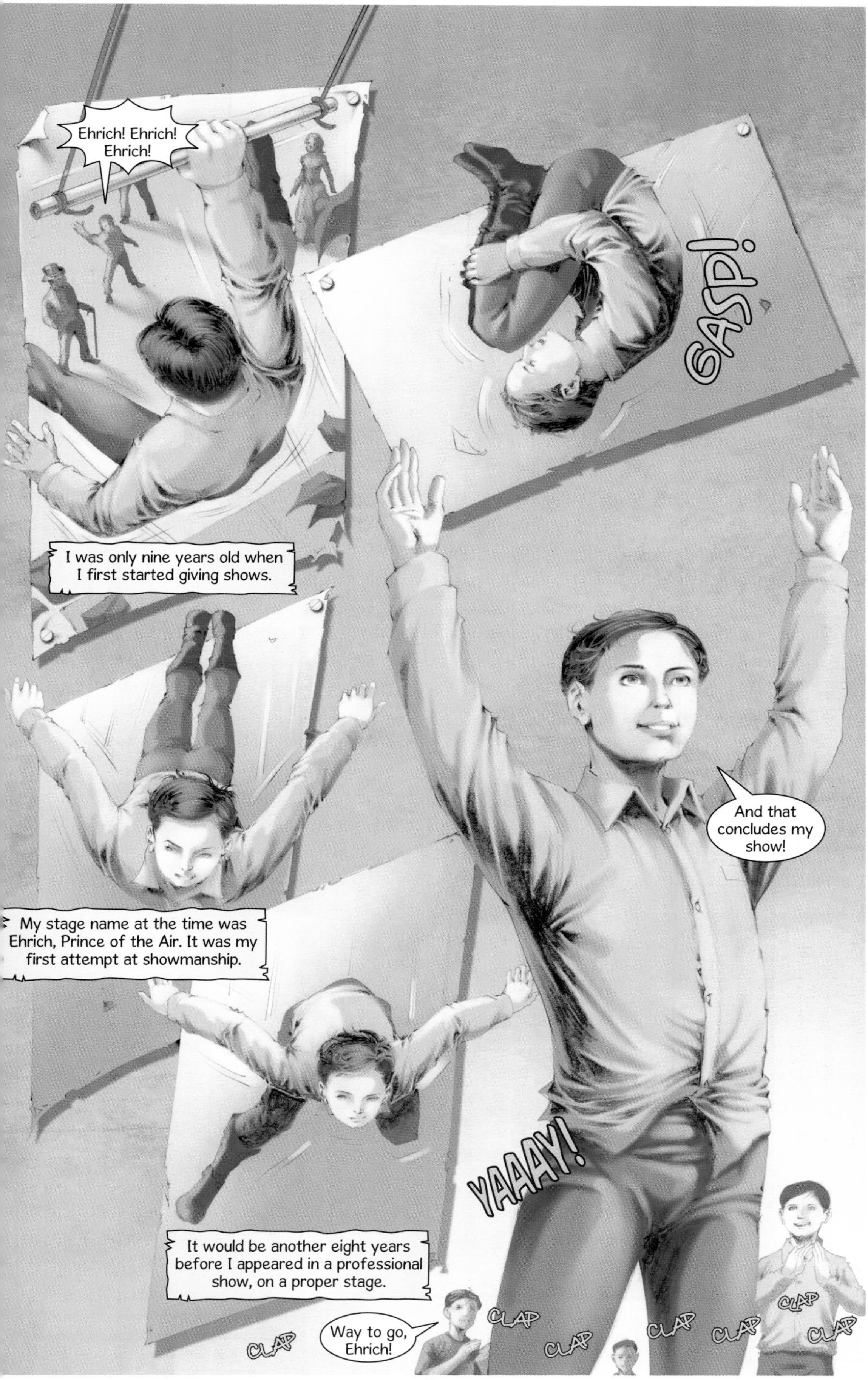
Ehrich! Ehrich! Ehrich!
GASP!
I was only nine years old when I first started giving shows.
My stage name at the time was Ehrich, Prince of the Air. It was my first attempt at showmanship.
And that concludes my show!
YAAAY!
It would be another eight years before I appeared in a professional show, on a proper stage.
Way to go, Ehrich!
CLAP
CLAP
CLAP
CLAP
CLAP
CLAP
CLAP

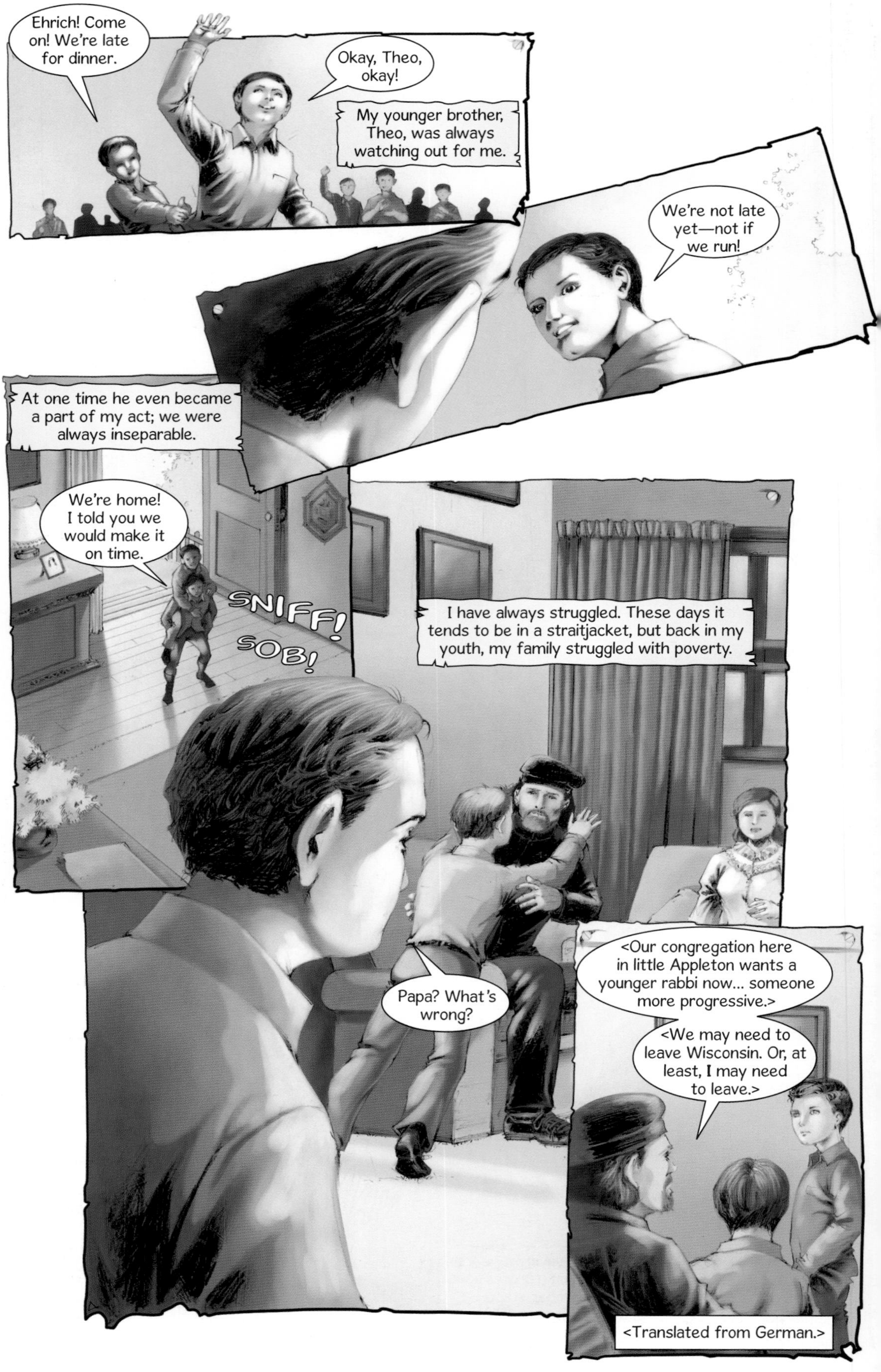

Ehrich! Come on! We're late for dinner.
Okay, Theo, okay!
My younger brother, Theo, was always watching out for me.
We're not late yet—not if we run!
At one time he even became a part of my act; we were always inseparable.
We're home! I told you we would make it on time.
SNIFFF!
SOB!
I have always struggled. These days it tends to be in a straitjacket, but back in my youth, my family struggled with poverty.
Papa? What's wrong?
<Our congregation here in little Appleton wants a younger rabbi now... someone more progressive.>
<We may need to leave Wisconsin. Or, at least, I may need to leave.>
<Translated from German.>

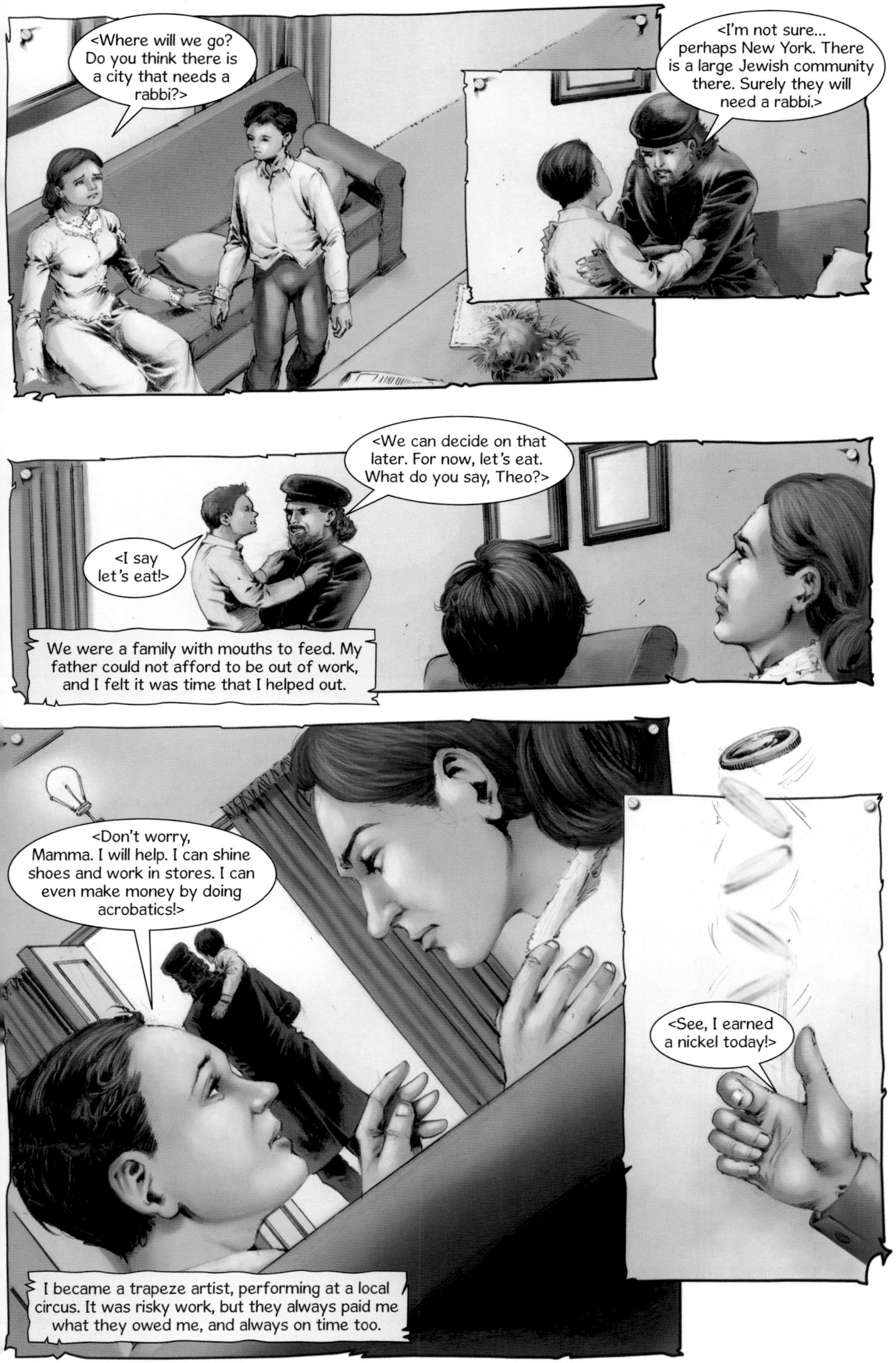
<Where will we go? Do you think there is a city that needs a rabbi?>
<I'm not sure... perhaps New York. There is a large Jewish community there. Surely they will need a rabbi.>
<We can decide on that later. For now, let's eat. What do you say, Theo?>
<I say let's eat!>
We were a family with mouths to feed. My father could not afford to be out of work, and I felt it was time that I helped out.
<Don't worry, Mamma. I will help. I can shine shoes and work in stores. I can even make money by doing acrobatics!>
<See, I earned a nickel today!>
I became a trapeze artist, performing at a local circus. It was risky work, but they always paid me what they owed me, and always on time too.

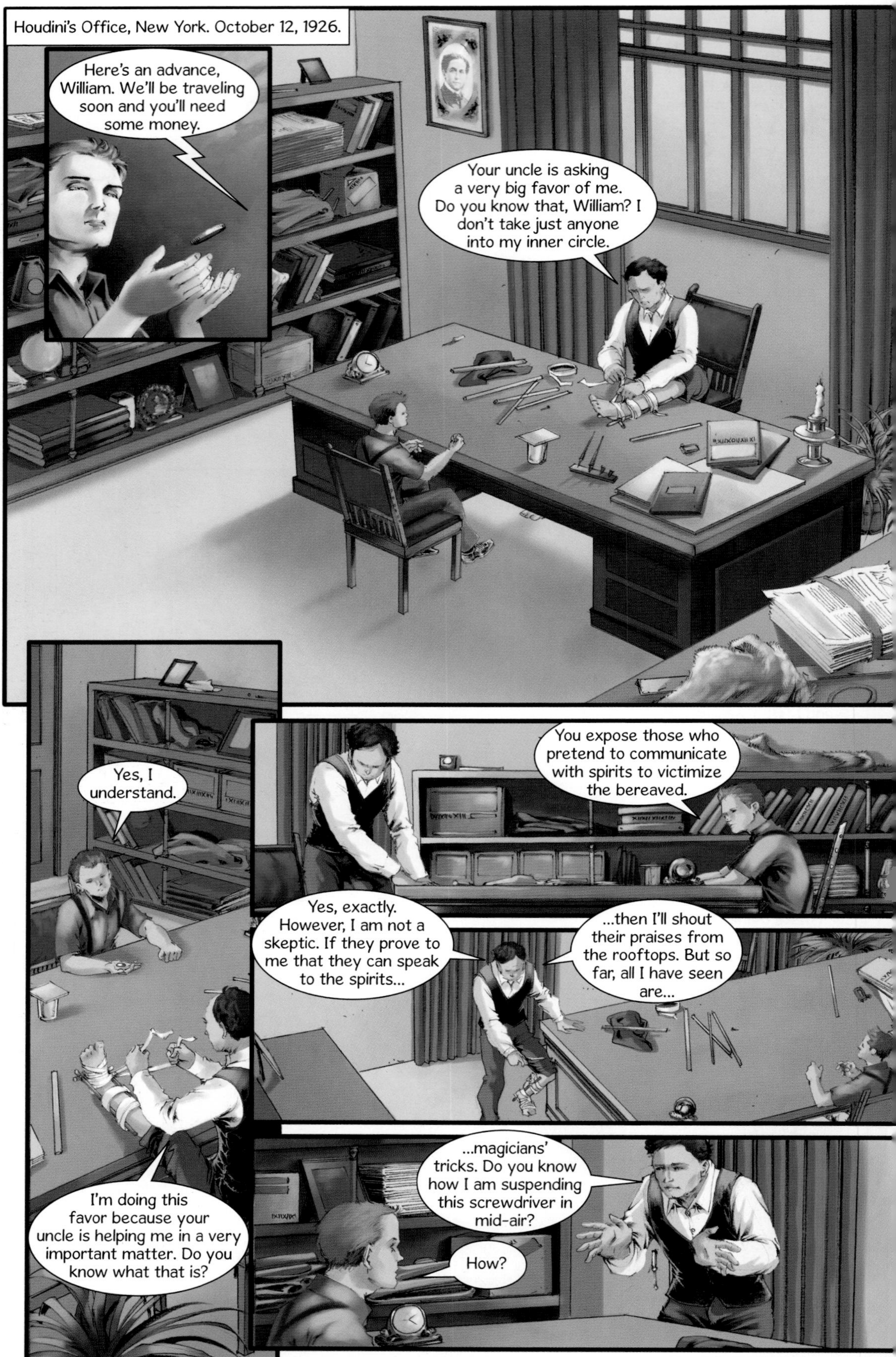
Houdini's Office, New York. October 12, 1926.
Here's an advance, William. We'll be traveling soon and you'll need some money.
Your uncle is asking a very big favor of me. Do you know that, William? I don't take just anyone into my inner circle.
Yes, I understand.
I'm doing this favor because your uncle is helping me in a very important matter. Do you know what that is?
You expose those who pretend to communicate with spirits to victimize the bereaved.
Yes, exactly. However, I am not a skeptic. If they prove to me that they can speak to the spirits...
...then I'll shout their praises from the rooftops. But so far, all I have seen are...
...magicians' tricks. Do you know how I am suspending this screwdriver in mid-air?
How?

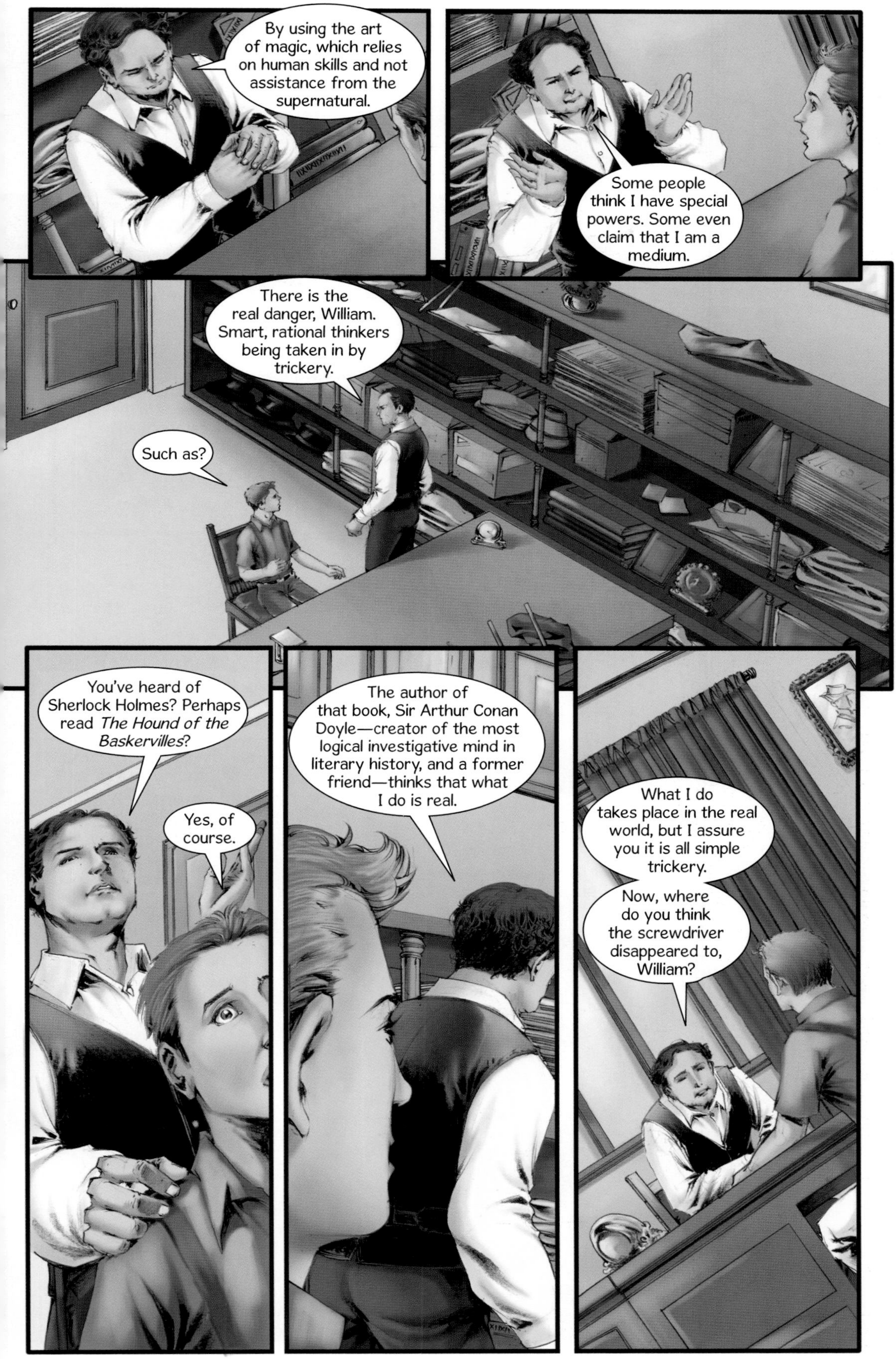
By using the art of magic, which relies on human skills and not assistance from the supernatural.
Some people think I have special powers. Some even claim that I am a medium.
There is the real danger, William. Smart, rational thinkers being taken in by trickery.
Such as?
You've heard of Sherlock Holmes? Perhaps read *The Hound of the Baskervilles*?
Yes, of course.
The author of that book, Sir Arthur Conan Doyle—creator of the most logical investigative mind in literary history, and a former friend—thinks that what I do is real.
What I do takes place in the real world, but I assure you it is all simple trickery.
Now, where do you think the screwdriver disappeared to, William?

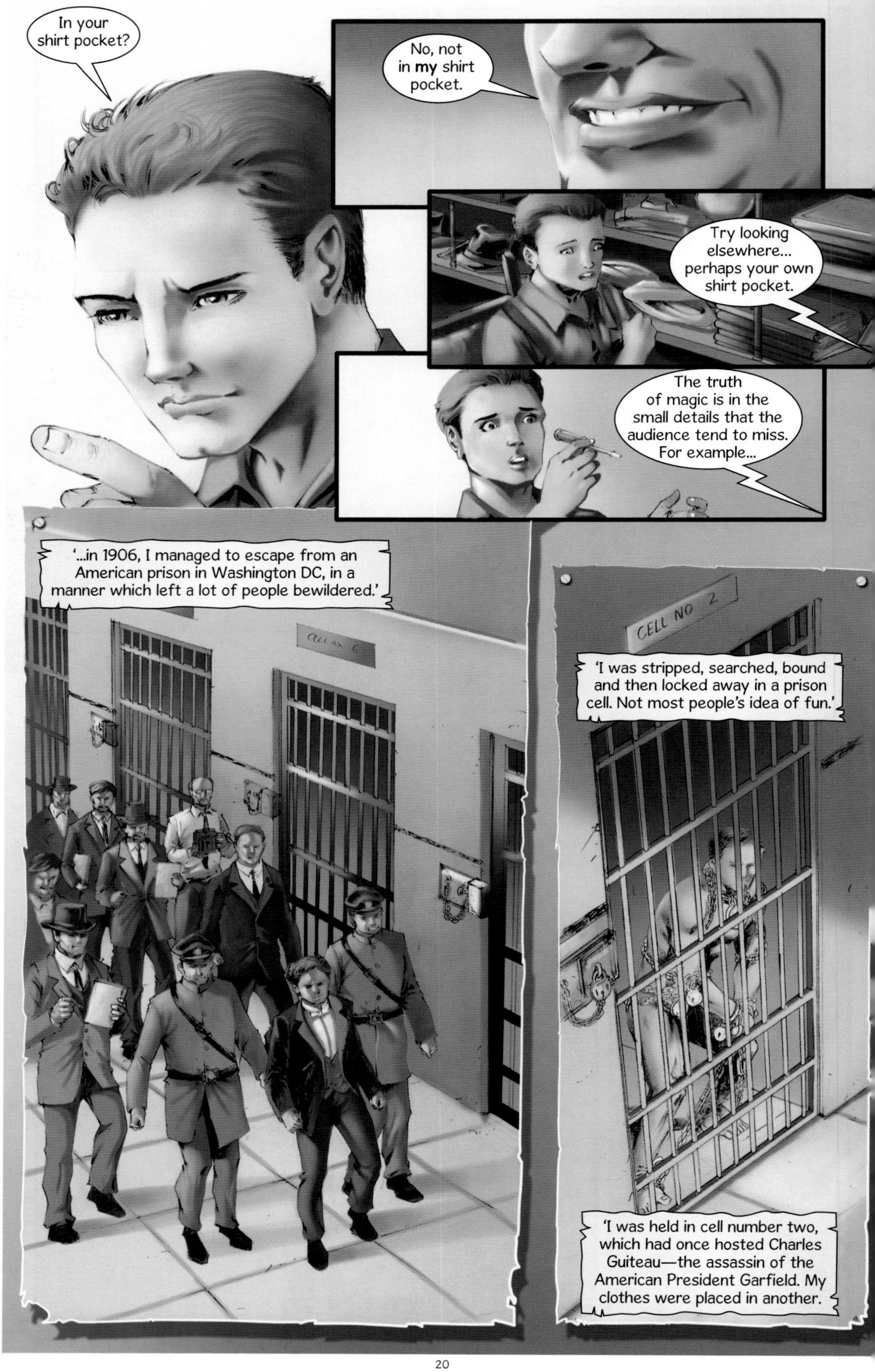
In your shirt pocket?
No, not in **my** shirt pocket.
Try looking elsewhere... perhaps your own shirt pocket.
The truth of magic is in the small details that the audience tend to miss. For example...
'...in 1906, I managed to escape from an American prison in Washington DC, in a manner which left a lot of people bewildered.'
CELL NO 2
'I was stripped, searched, bound and then locked away in a prison cell. Not most people's idea of fun.'
'I was held in cell number two, which had once hosted Charles Guiteau—the assassin of the American President Garfield. My clothes were placed in another.

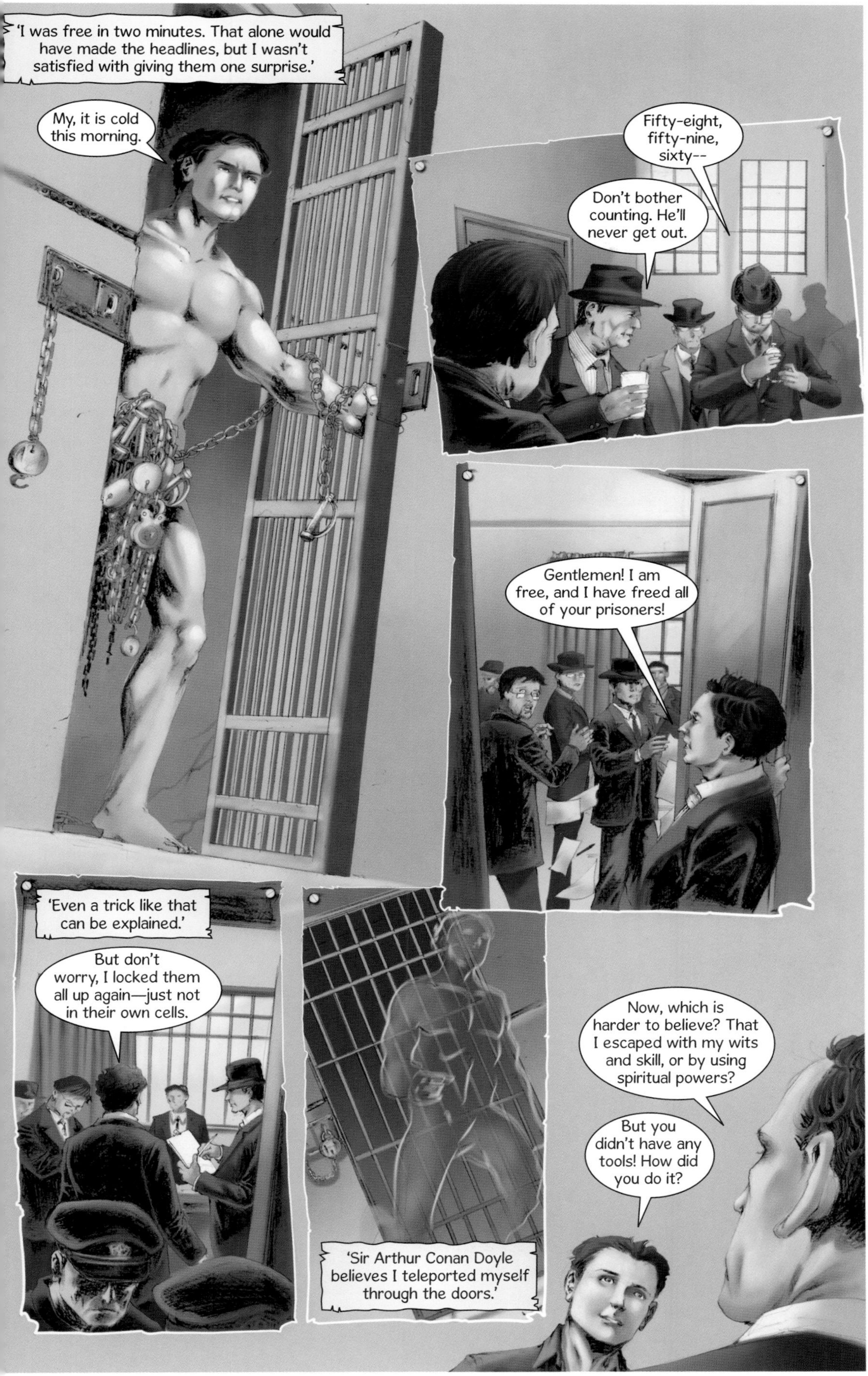
'I was free in two minutes. That alone would have made the headlines, but I wasn't satisfied with giving them one surprise.'
My, it is cold this morning.
Fifty-eight, fifty-nine, sixty--
Don't bother counting. He'll never get out.
Gentlemen! I am free, and I have freed all of your prisoners!
'Even a trick like that can be explained.'
But don't worry, I locked them all up again—just not in their own cells.
'Sir Arthur Conan Doyle believes I teleported myself through the doors.'
Now, which is harder to believe? That I escaped with my wits and skill, or by using spiritual powers?
But you didn't have any tools! How did you do it?

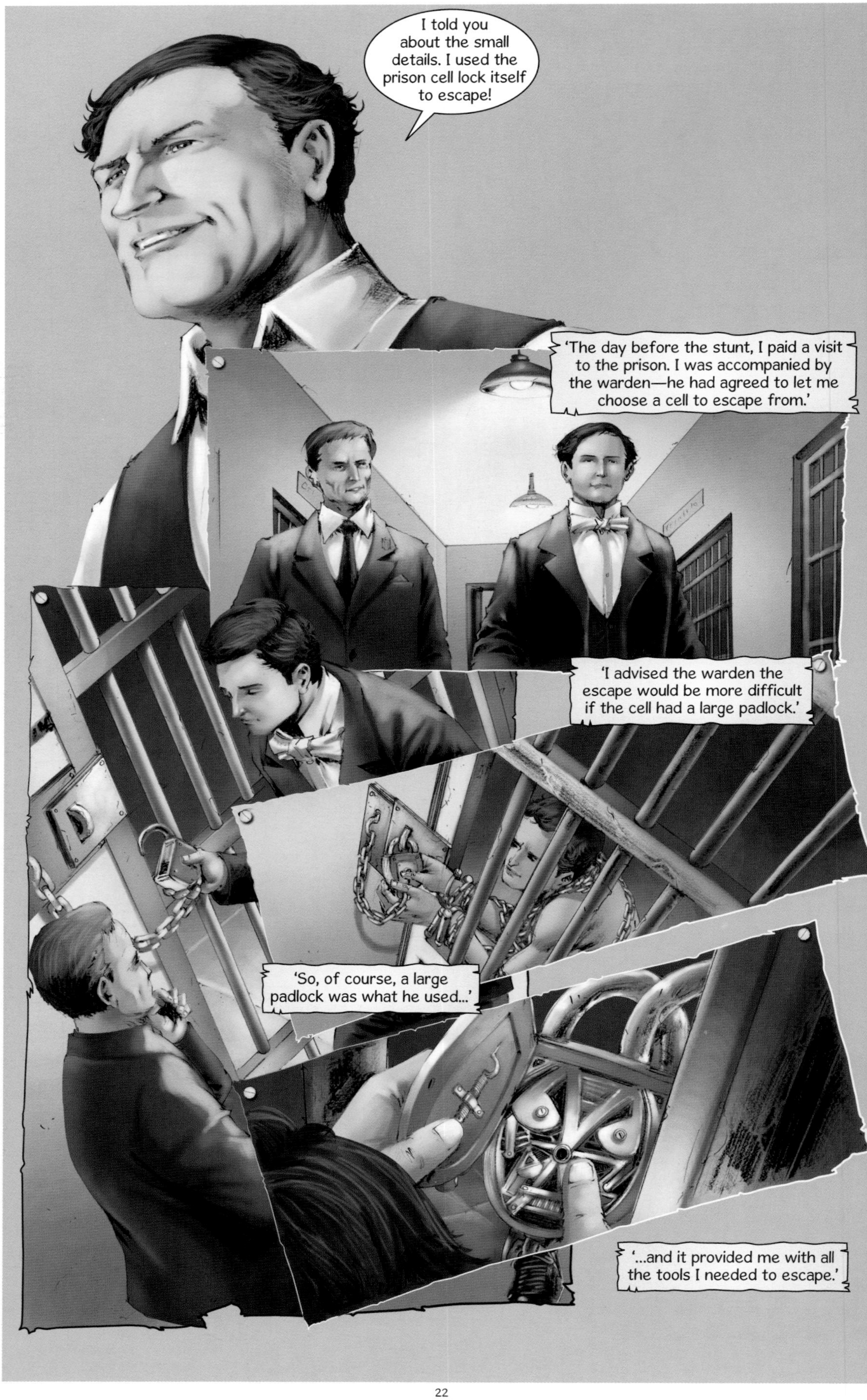
I told you about the small details. I used the prison cell lock itself to escape!
'The day before the stunt, I paid a visit to the prison. I was accompanied by the warden—he had agreed to let me choose a cell to escape from.'
'I advised the warden the escape would be more difficult if the cell had a large padlock.'
'So, of course, a large padlock was what he used...'
'...and it provided me with all the tools I needed to escape.'

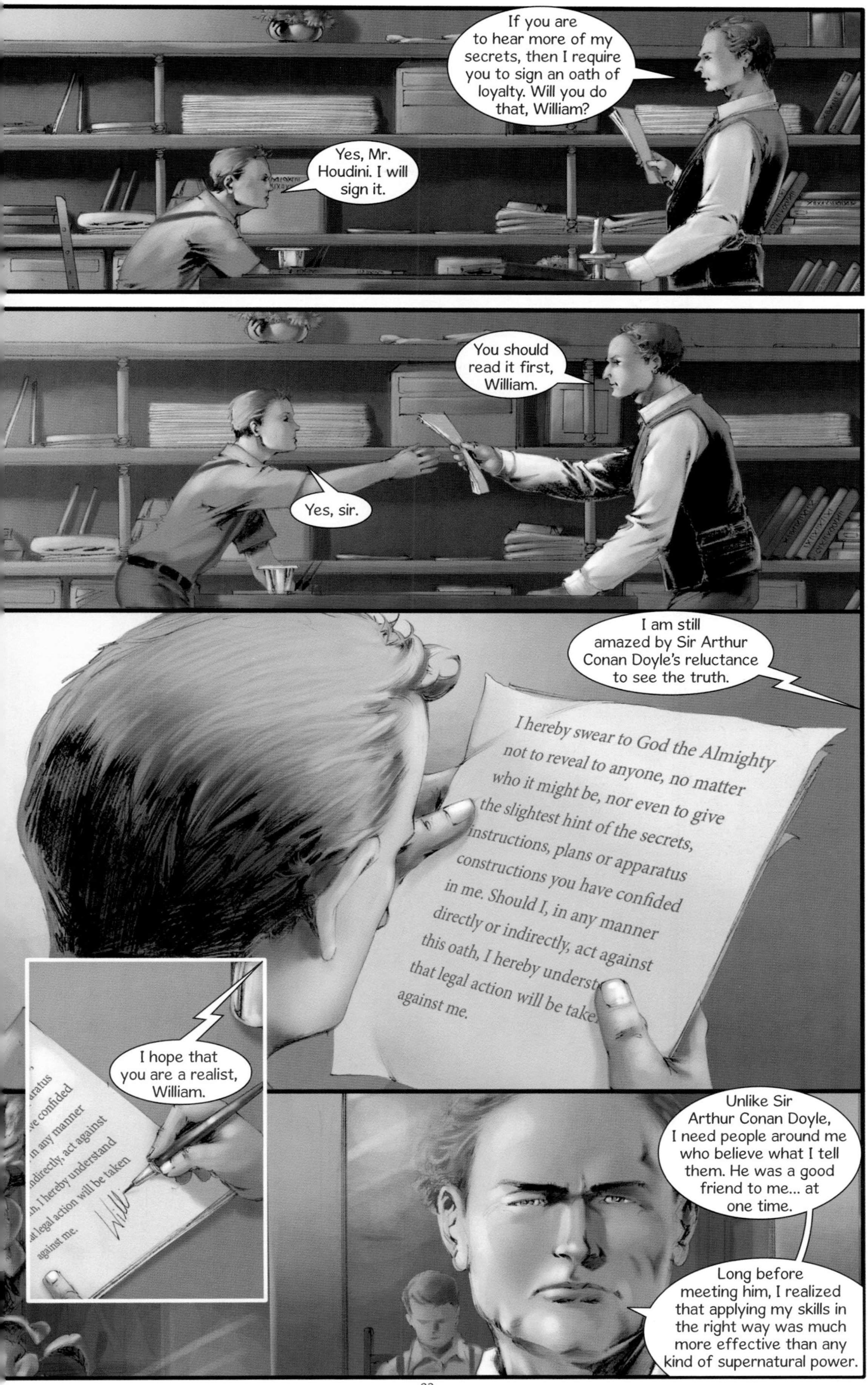
If you are to hear more of my secrets, then I require you to sign an oath of loyalty. Will you do that, William?
Yes, Mr. Houdini. I will sign it.
You should read it first, William.
Yes, sir.
I am still amazed by Sir Arthur Conan Doyle's reluctance to see the truth.
I hereby swear to God the Almighty not to reveal to anyone, no matter who it might be, nor even to give the slightest hint of the secrets, instructions, plans or apparatus constructions you have confided in me. Should I, in any manner directly or indirectly, act against this oath, I hereby underst... that legal action will be take... against me.
I hope that you are a realist, William.
Unlike Sir Arthur Conan Doyle, I need people around me who believe what I tell them. He was a good friend to me... at one time.
Long before meeting him, I realized that applying my skills in the right way was much more effective than any kind of supernatural power.

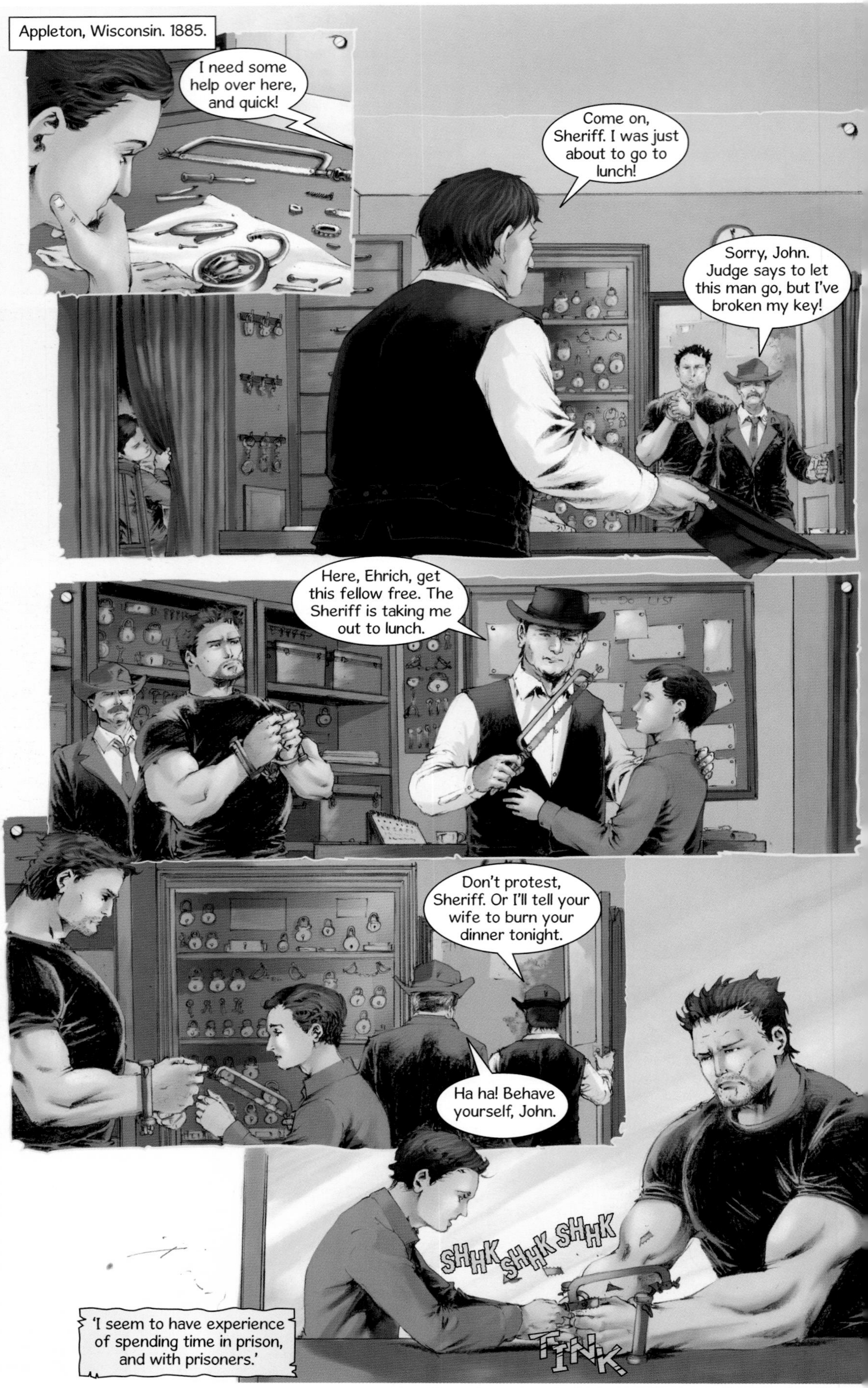

Appleton, Wisconsin. 1885.
I need some help over here, and quick!
Come on, Sheriff. I was just about to go to lunch!
Sorry, John. Judge says to let this man go, but I've broken my key!
Here, Ehrich, get this fellow free. The Sheriff is taking me out to lunch.
Don't protest, Sheriff. Or I'll tell your wife to burn your dinner tonight.
Ha ha! Behave yourself, John.
SHHK SHHK SHHK
'I seem to have experience of spending time in prison, and with prisoners.'
TINK

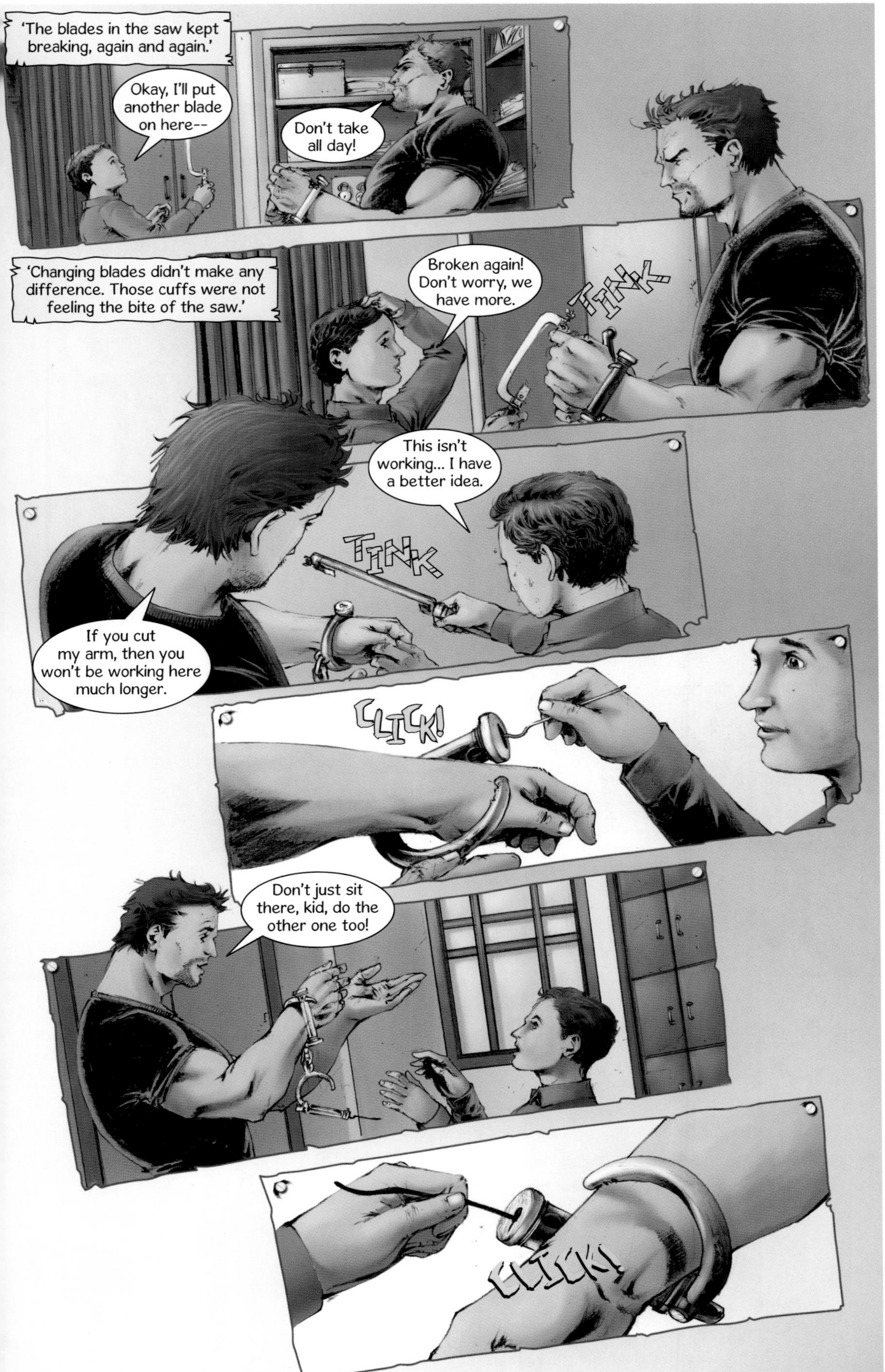

'The blades in the saw kept breaking, again and again.'
Okay, I'll put another blade on here--
Don't take all day!
'Changing blades didn't make any difference. Those cuffs were not feeling the bite of the saw.'
Broken again! Don't worry, we have more.
TINK
This isn't working... I have a better idea.
TINK
If you cut my arm, then you won't be working here much longer.
CLICK!
Don't just sit there, kid, do the other one too!
CLICK!

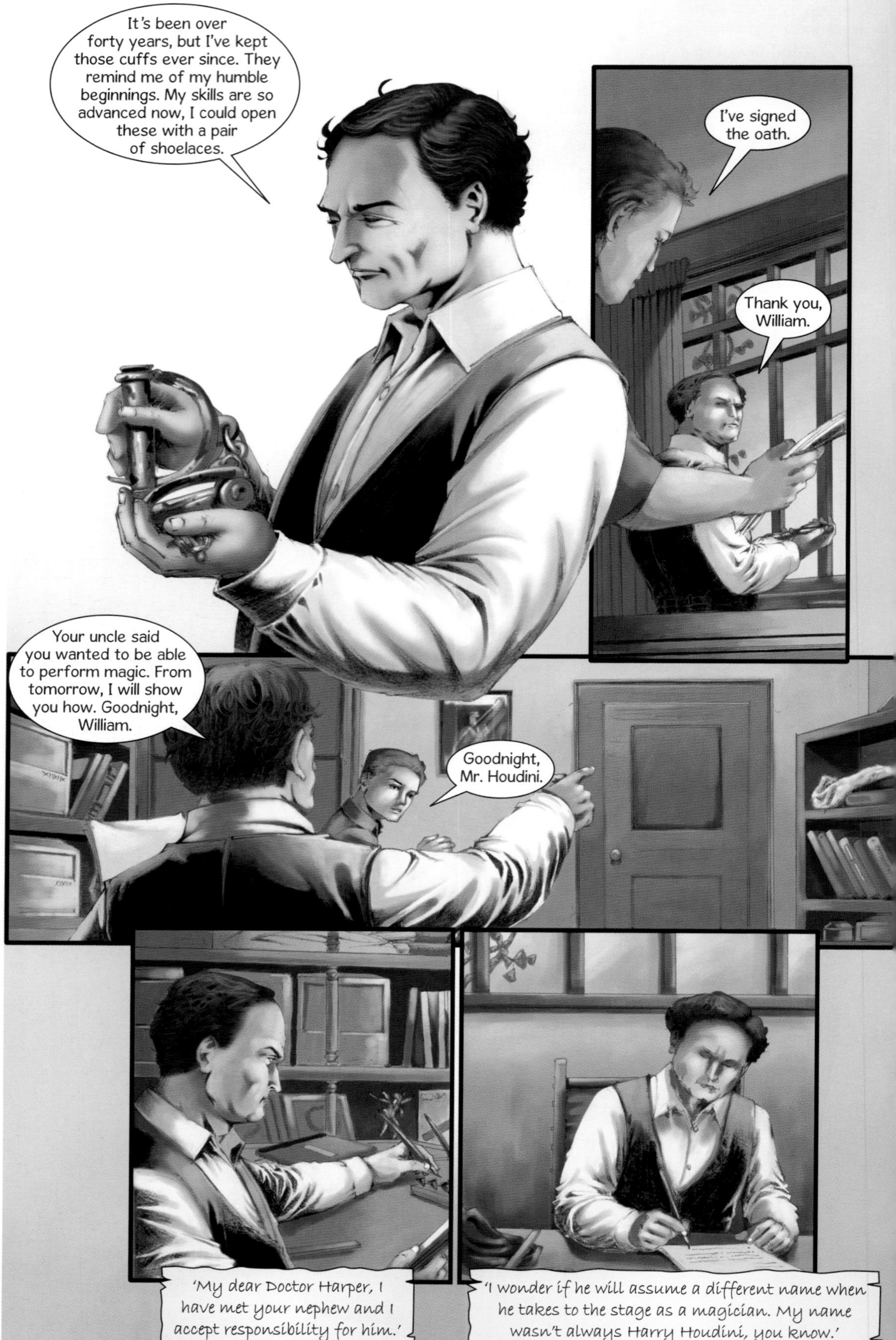
It's been over forty years, but I've kept those cuffs ever since. They remind me of my humble beginnings. My skills are so advanced now, I could open these with a pair of shoelaces.
I've signed the oath.
Thank you, William.
Your uncle said you wanted to be able to perform magic. From tomorrow, I will show you how. Goodnight, William.
Goodnight, Mr. Houdini.
'My dear Doctor Harper, I have met your nephew and I accept responsibility for him.'
'I wonder if he will assume a different name when he takes to the stage as a magician. My name wasn't always Harry Houdini, you know.'

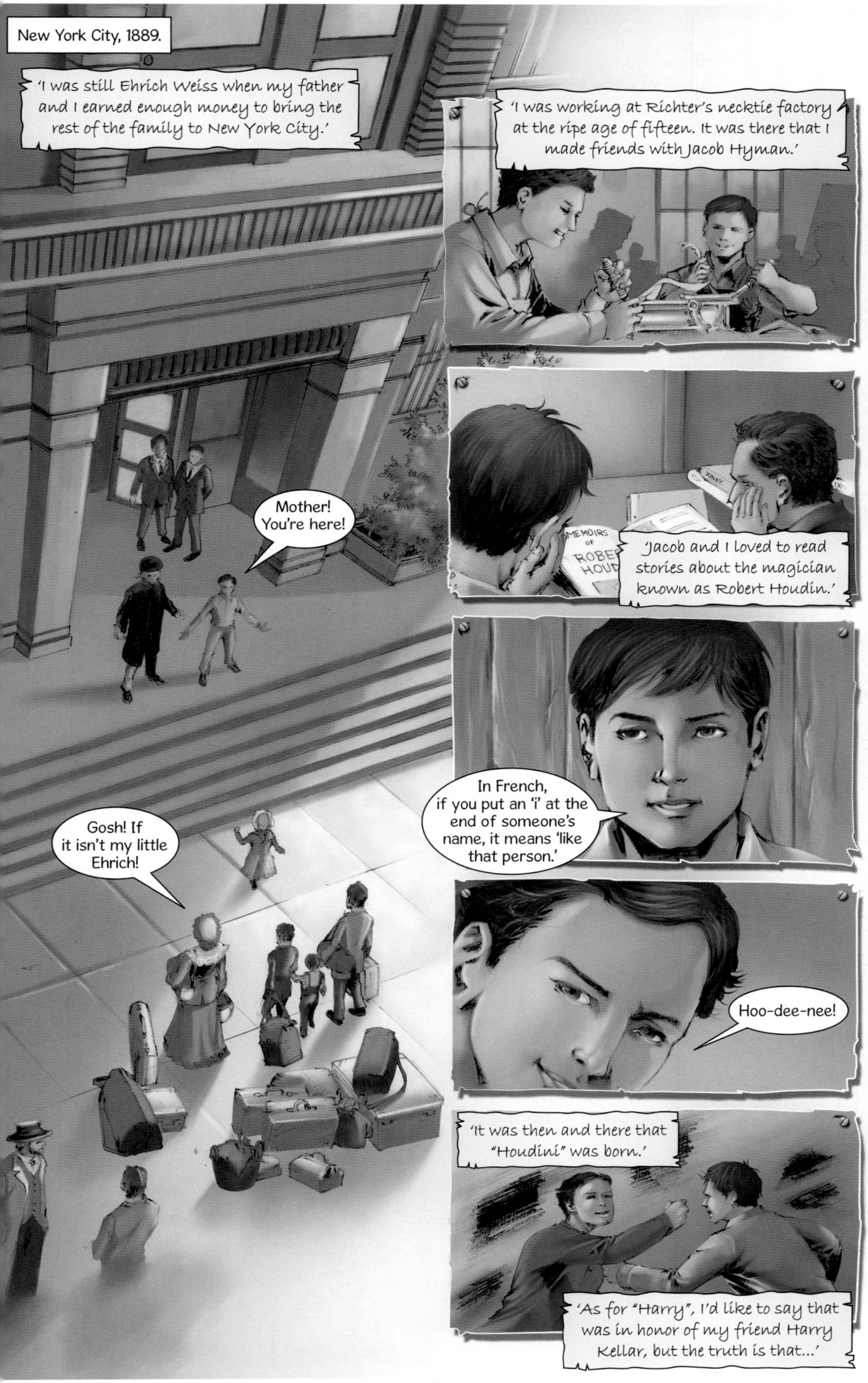
New York City, 1889.
'I was still Ehrich Weiss when my father and I earned enough money to bring the rest of the family to New York City.'
Mother! You're here!
Gosh! If it isn't my little Ehrich!
'I was working at Richter's necktie factory at the ripe age of fifteen. It was there that I made friends with Jacob Hyman.'
'Jacob and I loved to read stories about the magician known as Robert Houdin.'
In French, if you put an 'i' at the end of someone's name, it means 'like that person.'
Hoo-dee-nee!
'It was then and there that "Houdini" was born.'
'As for "Harry", I'd like to say that was in honor of my friend Harry Kellar, but the truth is that...'

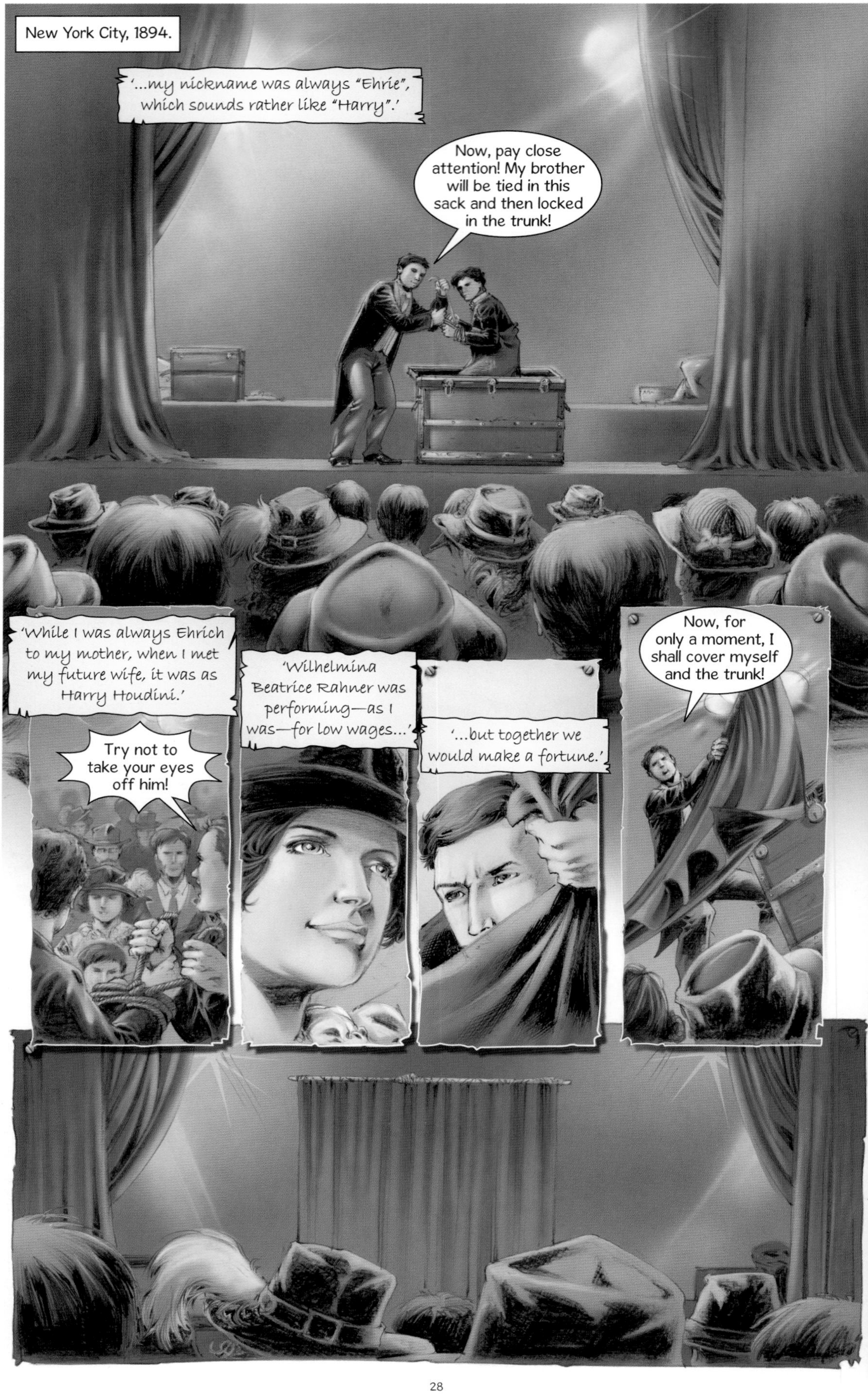
New York City, 1894.
'...my nickname was always "Ehrie", which sounds rather like "Harry".'
Now, pay close attention! My brother will be tied in this sack and then locked in the trunk!
'While I was always Ehrich to my mother, when I met my future wife, it was as Harry Houdini.'
Try not to take your eyes off him!
'Wilhelmina Beatrice Rahner was performing—as I was—for low wages...'
'...but together we would make a fortune.'
Now, for only a moment, I shall cover myself and the trunk!

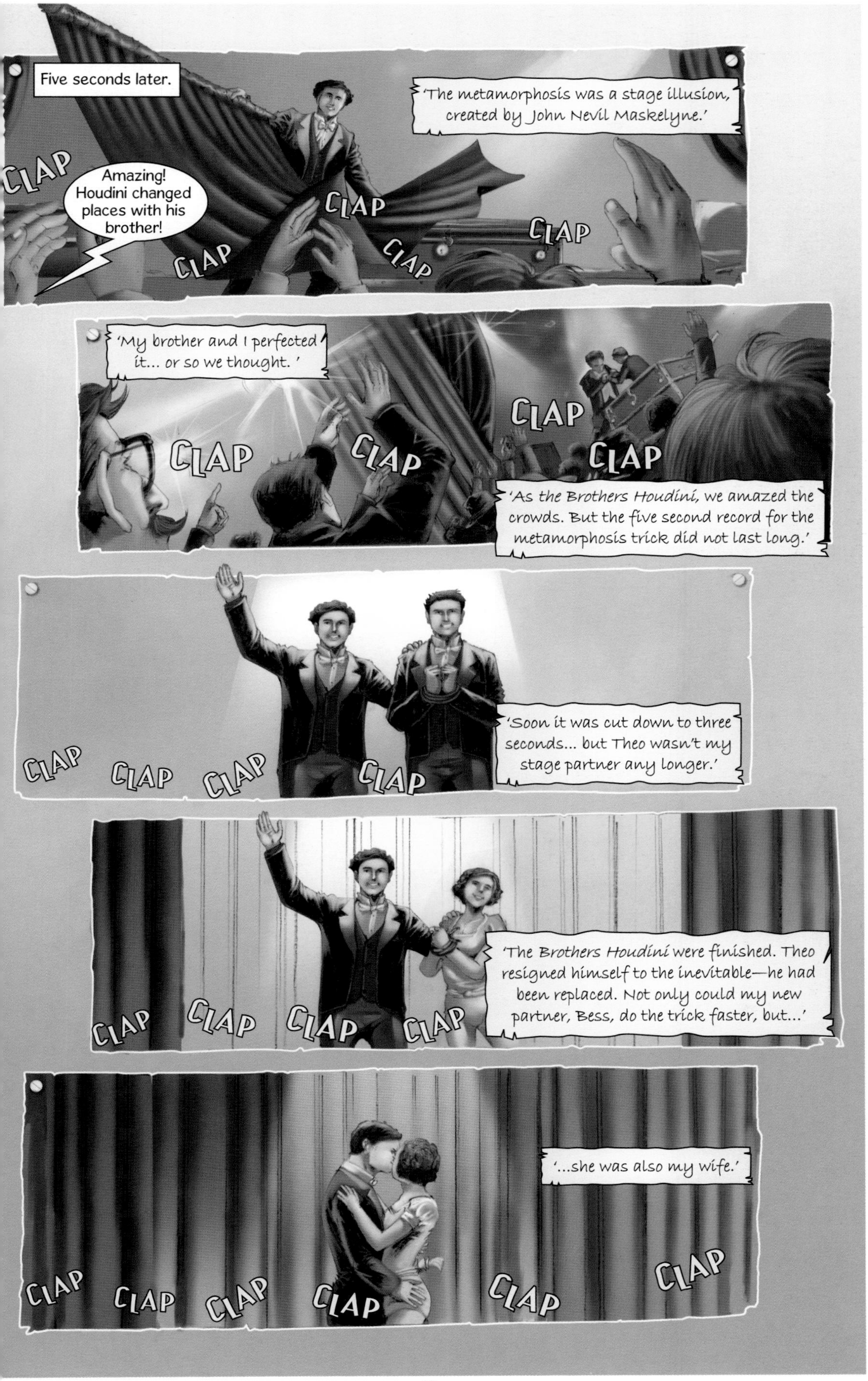
Five seconds later.
'The metamorphosis was a stage illusion, created by John Nevil Maskelyne.'
CLAP
Amazing! Houdini changed places with his brother!
CLAP
CLAP
CLAP
CLAP
'My brother and I perfected it... or so we thought.'
CLAP
CLAP
CLAP
CLAP
'As the Brothers Houdini, we amazed the crowds. But the five second record for the metamorphosis trick did not last long.'
CLAP
CLAP
CLAP
CLAP
'Soon it was cut down to three seconds... but Theo wasn't my stage partner any longer.'
CLAP
CLAP
CLAP
CLAP
'The Brothers Houdini were finished. Theo resigned himself to the inevitable—he had been replaced. Not only could my new partner, Bess, do the trick faster, but...'
'...she was also my wife.'
CLAP
CLAP
CLAP
CLAP
CLAP
CLAP

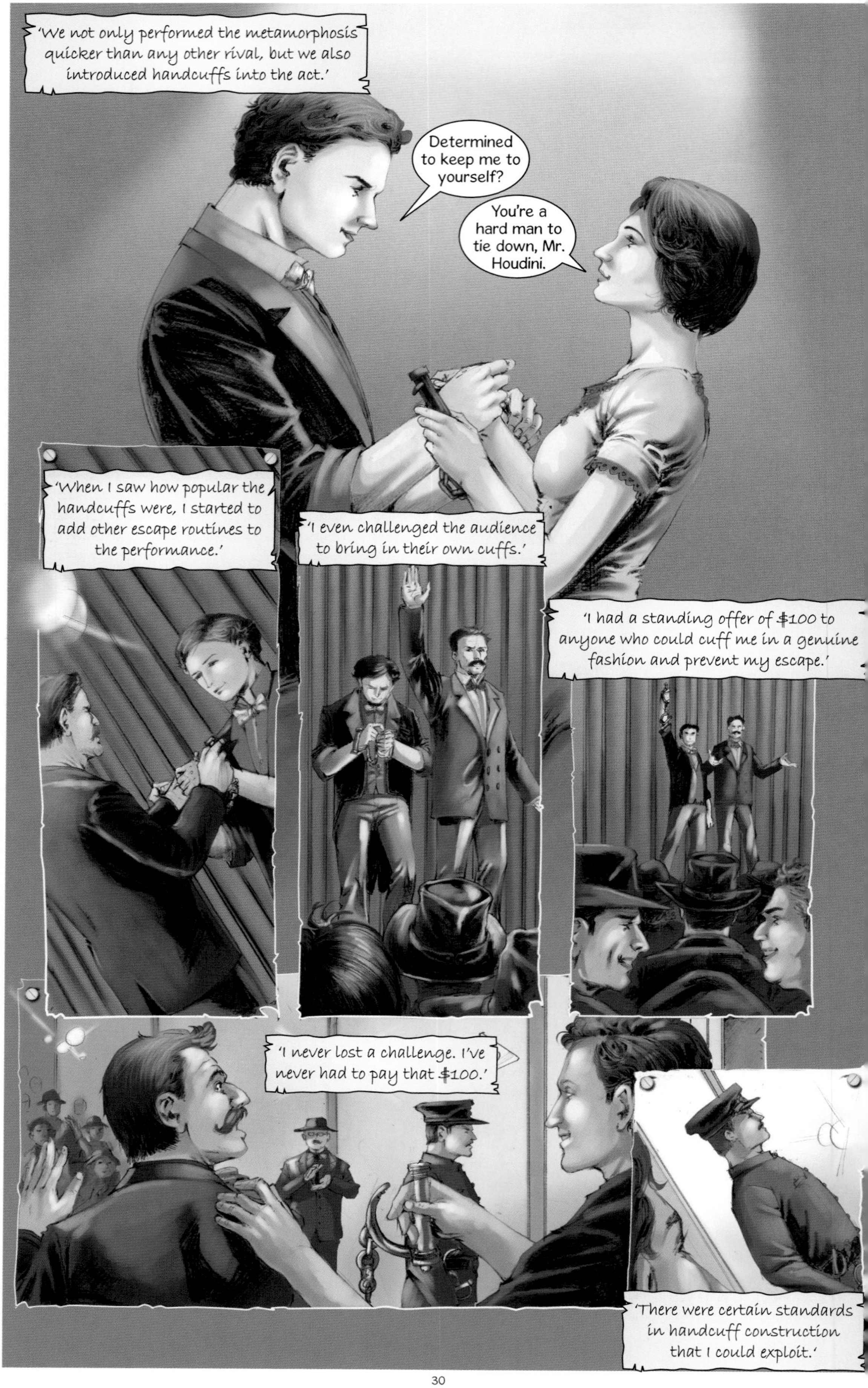
'We not only performed the metamorphosis quicker than any other rival, but we also introduced handcuffs into the act.'
Determined to keep me to yourself?
You're a hard man to tie down, Mr. Houdini.
'When I saw how popular the handcuffs were, I started to add other escape routines to the performance.'
'I even challenged the audience to bring in their own cuffs.'
'I had a standing offer of $100 to anyone who could cuff me in a genuine fashion and prevent my escape.'
'I never lost a challenge. I've never had to pay that $100.'
'There were certain standards in handcuff construction that I could exploit.'

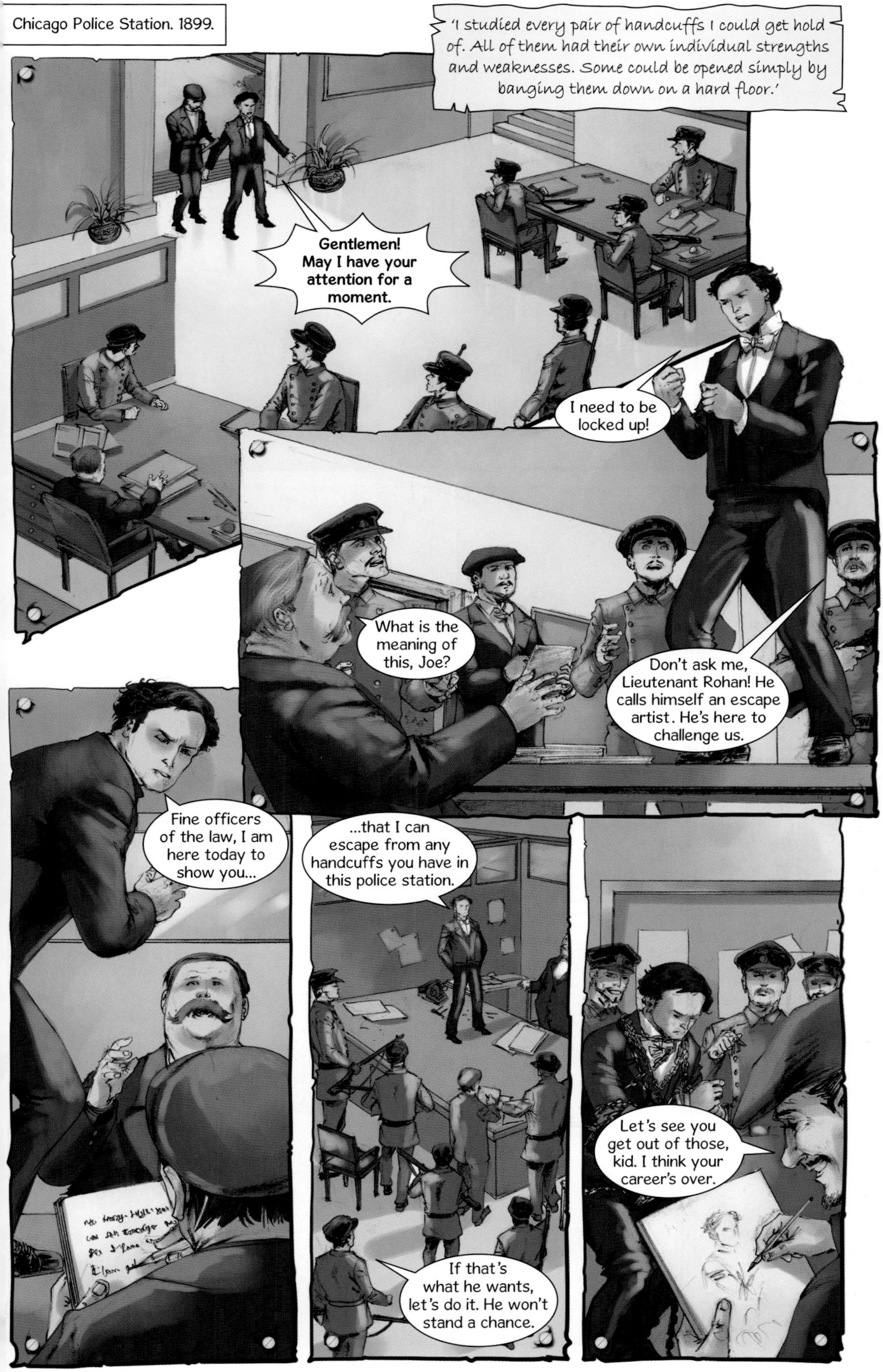
Chicago Police Station. 1899.
'I studied every pair of handcuffs I could get hold of. All of them had their own individual strengths and weaknesses. Some could be opened simply by banging them down on a hard floor.'
Gentlemen! May I have your attention for a moment.
I need to be locked up!
What is the meaning of this, Joe?
Don't ask me, Lieutenant Rohan! He calls himself an escape artist. He's here to challenge us.
Fine officers of the law, I am here today to show you...
...that I can escape from any handcuffs you have in this police station.
If that's what he wants, let's do it. He won't stand a chance.
Let's see you get out of those, kid. I think your career's over.

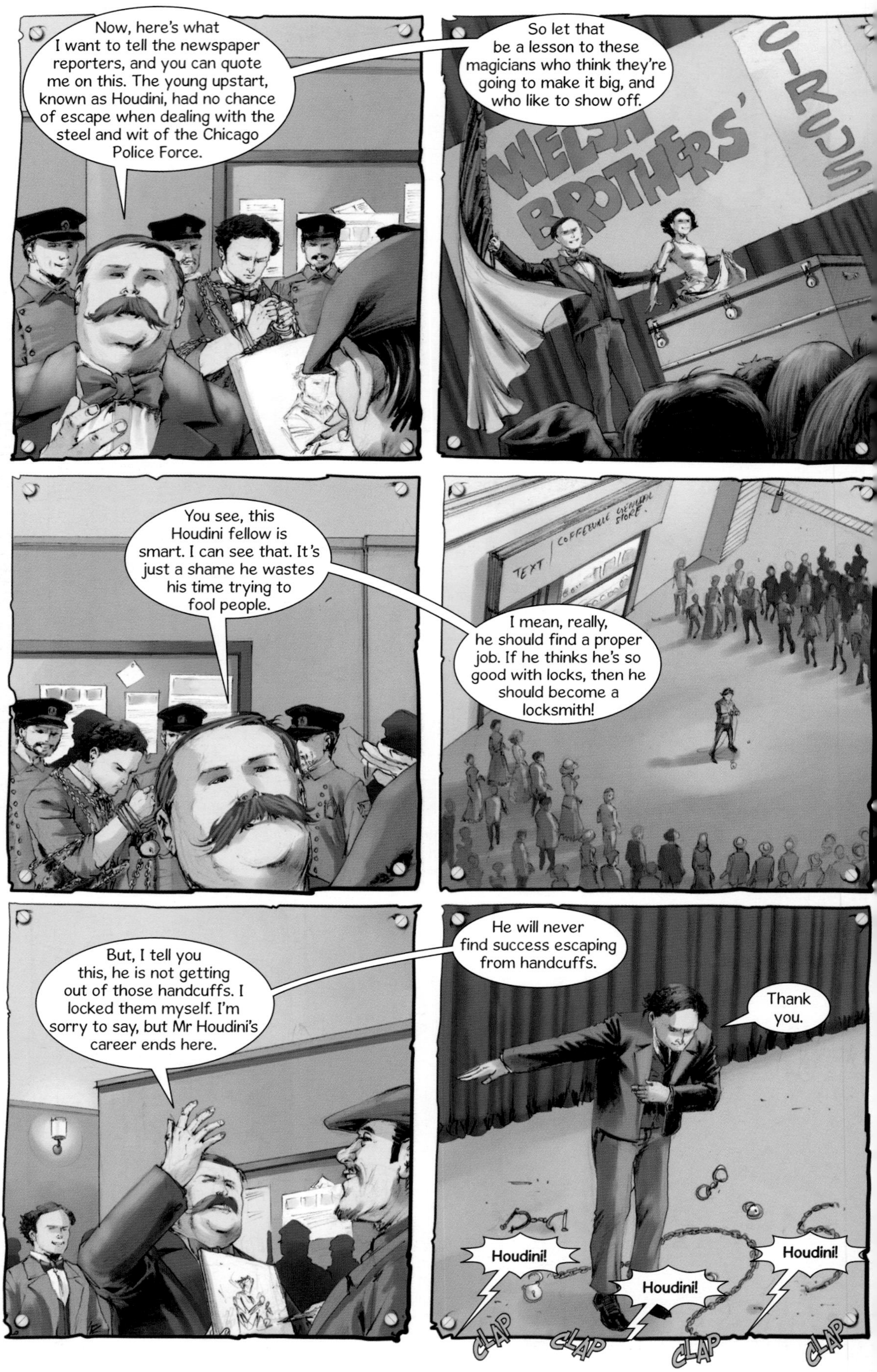
Now, here's what I want to tell the newspaper reporters, and you can quote me on this. The young upstart, known as Houdini, had no chance of escape when dealing with the steel and wit of the Chicago Police Force.
So let that be a lesson to these magicians who think they're going to make it big, and who like to show off.
BROTHERS'
CIRCUS
You see, this Houdini fellow is smart. I can see that. It's just a shame he wastes his time trying to fool people.
I mean, really, he should find a proper job. If he thinks he's so good with locks, then he should become a locksmith!
But, I tell you this, he is not getting out of those handcuffs. I locked them myself. I'm sorry to say, but Mr Houdini's career ends here.
He will never find success escaping from handcuffs.
Thank you.
Houdini!
Houdini!
Houdini!
CLAP
CLAP
CLAP
CLAP

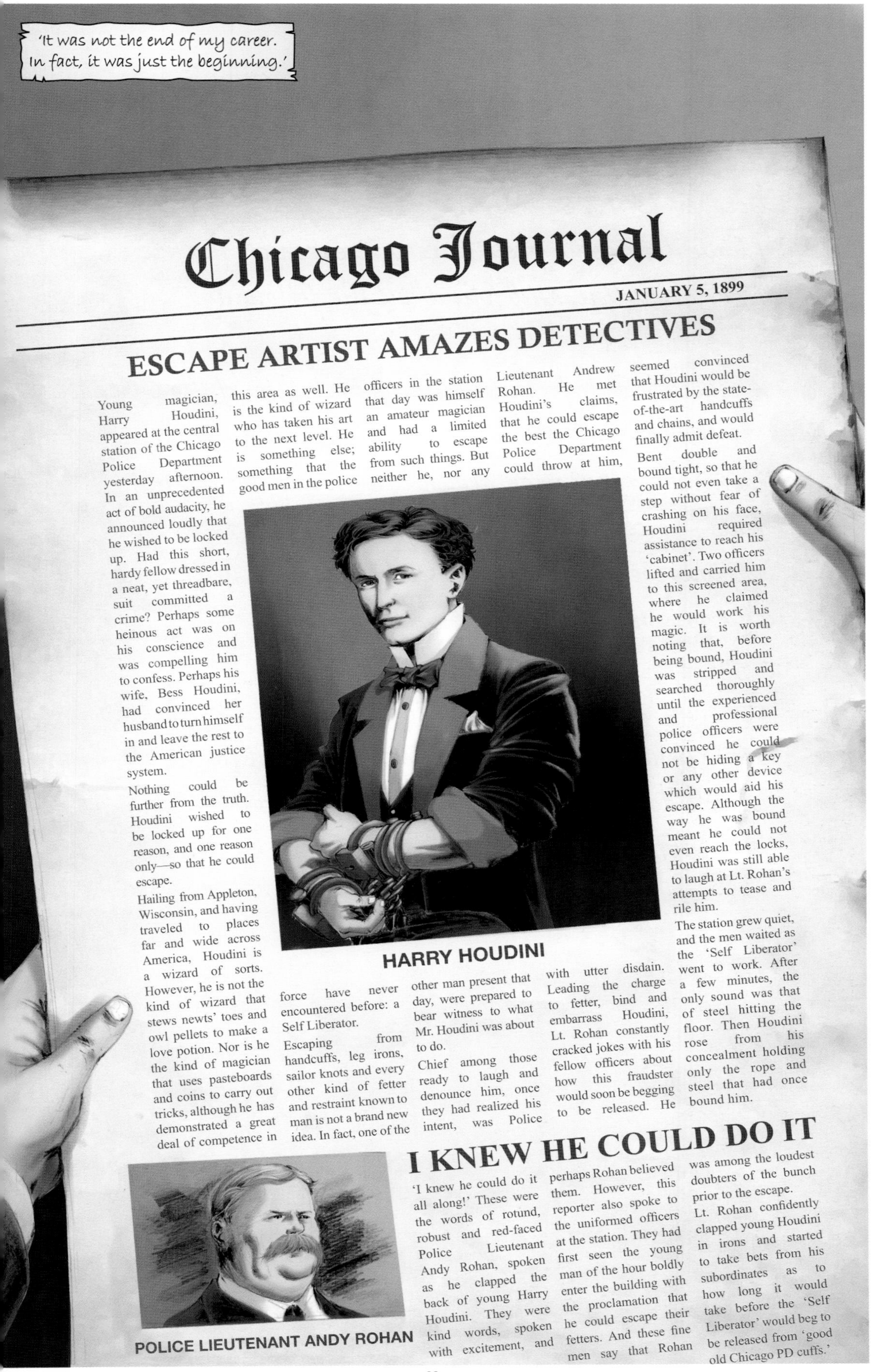
'It was not the end of my career. In fact, it was just the beginning.'

# Chicago Journal

JANUARY 5, 1899

## ESCAPE ARTIST AMAZES DETECTIVES

Young magician, Harry Houdini, appeared at the central station of the Chicago Police Department yesterday afternoon. In an unprecedented act of bold audacity, he announced loudly that he wished to be locked up. Had this short, hardy fellow dressed in a neat, yet threadbare, suit committed a crime? Perhaps some heinous act was on his conscience and was compelling him to confess. Perhaps his wife, Bess Houdini, had convinced her husband to turn himself in and leave the rest to the American justice system.

Nothing could be further from the truth. Houdini wished to be locked up for one reason, and one reason only—so that he could escape.

Hailing from Appleton, Wisconsin, and having traveled to places far and wide across America, Houdini is a wizard of sorts. However, he is not the kind of wizard that stews newts' toes and owl pellets to make a love potion. Nor is he the kind of magician that uses pasteboards and coins to carry out tricks, although he has demonstrated a great deal of competence in this area as well. He is the kind of wizard who has taken his art to the next level. He is something else; something that the good men in the police force have never encountered before: a Self Liberator.

Escaping from handcuffs, leg irons, sailor knots and every other kind of fetter and restraint known to man is not a brand new idea. In fact, one of the officers in the station that day was himself an amateur magician and had a limited ability to escape from such things. But neither he, nor any other man present that day, were prepared to bear witness to what Mr. Houdini was about to do.

Chief among those ready to laugh and denounce him, once they had realized his intent, was Police Lieutenant Andrew Rohan. He met Houdini's claims, that he could escape the best the Chicago Police Department could throw at him, with utter disdain. Leading the charge to fetter, bind and embarrass Houdini, Lt. Rohan constantly cracked jokes with his fellow officers about how this fraudster would soon be begging to be released. He seemed convinced that Houdini would be frustrated by the state-of-the-art handcuffs and chains, and would finally admit defeat.

Bent double and bound tight, so that he could not even take a step without fear of crashing on his face, Houdini required assistance to reach his 'cabinet'. Two officers lifted and carried him to this screened area, where he claimed he would work his magic. It is worth noting that, before being bound, Houdini was stripped and searched thoroughly until the experienced and professional police officers were convinced he could not be hiding a key or any other device which would aid his escape. Although the way he was bound meant he could not even reach the locks, Houdini was still able to laugh at Lt. Rohan's attempts to tease and rile him.

The station grew quiet, and the men waited as the 'Self Liberator' went to work. After a few minutes, the only sound was that of steel hitting the floor. Then Houdini rose from his concealment holding only the rope and steel that had once bound him.

HARRY HOUDINI

## I KNEW HE COULD DO IT

'I knew he could do it all along!' These were the words of rotund, robust and red-faced Police Lieutenant Andy Rohan, spoken as he clapped the back of young Harry Houdini. They were kind words, spoken with excitement, and perhaps Rohan believed them. However, this reporter also spoke to the uniformed officers at the station. They had first seen the young man of the hour boldly enter the building with the proclamation that he could escape their fetters. And these fine men say that Rohan was among the loudest doubters of the bunch prior to the escape. Lt. Rohan confidently clapped young Houdini in irons and started to take bets from his subordinates as to how long it would take before the 'Self Liberator' would beg to be released from 'good old Chicago PD cuffs.'

POLICE LIEUTENANT ANDY ROHAN

*October 13, 1926*

*I have done some preliminary research on my friend, Harry Houdini, and found out the following:*

*After his escape from the chains and cuffs of the Chicago Police Force in 1899, he spent the following years earning a reputation around the world for daring feats—escaping from shackles, handcuffs, ropes and various locked containers such as coffins, milk cans and prison cells.*

*Once, in an outdoor exhibition, he allowed himself to be suspended more than seventy-five feet in the air, upside down, while he amazed onlookers by freeing himself from a straitjacket.*

October 13, 1926 (Continued)

Always one for showing how multi-talented he was, in 1909, Houdini purchased a French 'Voisin' biplane for five thousand dollars. In it, he achieved the first controlled, powered flight over Australia on March 21, 1910.

Houdini even found time to act in several motion pictures from 1916 through 1923.

As I well know, Houdini has spent the last few years, not only continuing to defy death with his escape routines, but also campaigning against mind readers, mediums and anyone who claims to have supernatural powers.

He claims they are all frauds, and has proven time and again that many of them fake their powers with elaborate tricks.

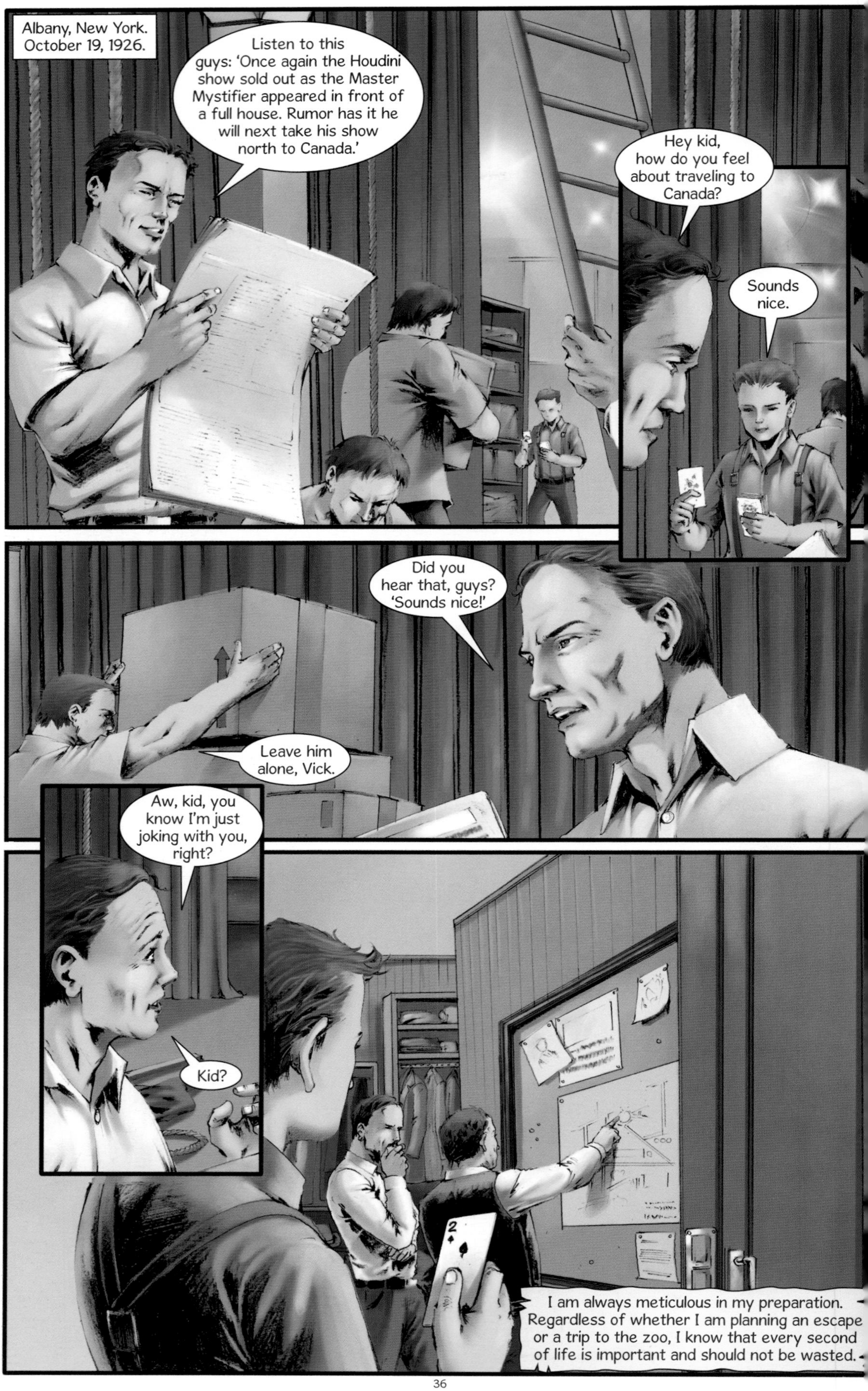
Albany, New York. October 19, 1926.
Listen to this guys: 'Once again the Houdini show sold out as the Master Mystifier appeared in front of a full house. Rumor has it he will next take his show north to Canada.'
Hey kid, how do you feel about traveling to Canada?
Sounds nice.
Did you hear that, guys? 'Sounds nice!'
Leave him alone, Vick.
Aw, kid, you know I'm just joking with you, right?
Kid?
I am always meticulous in my preparation. Regardless of whether I am planning an escape or a trip to the zoo, I know that every second of life is important and should not be wasted.

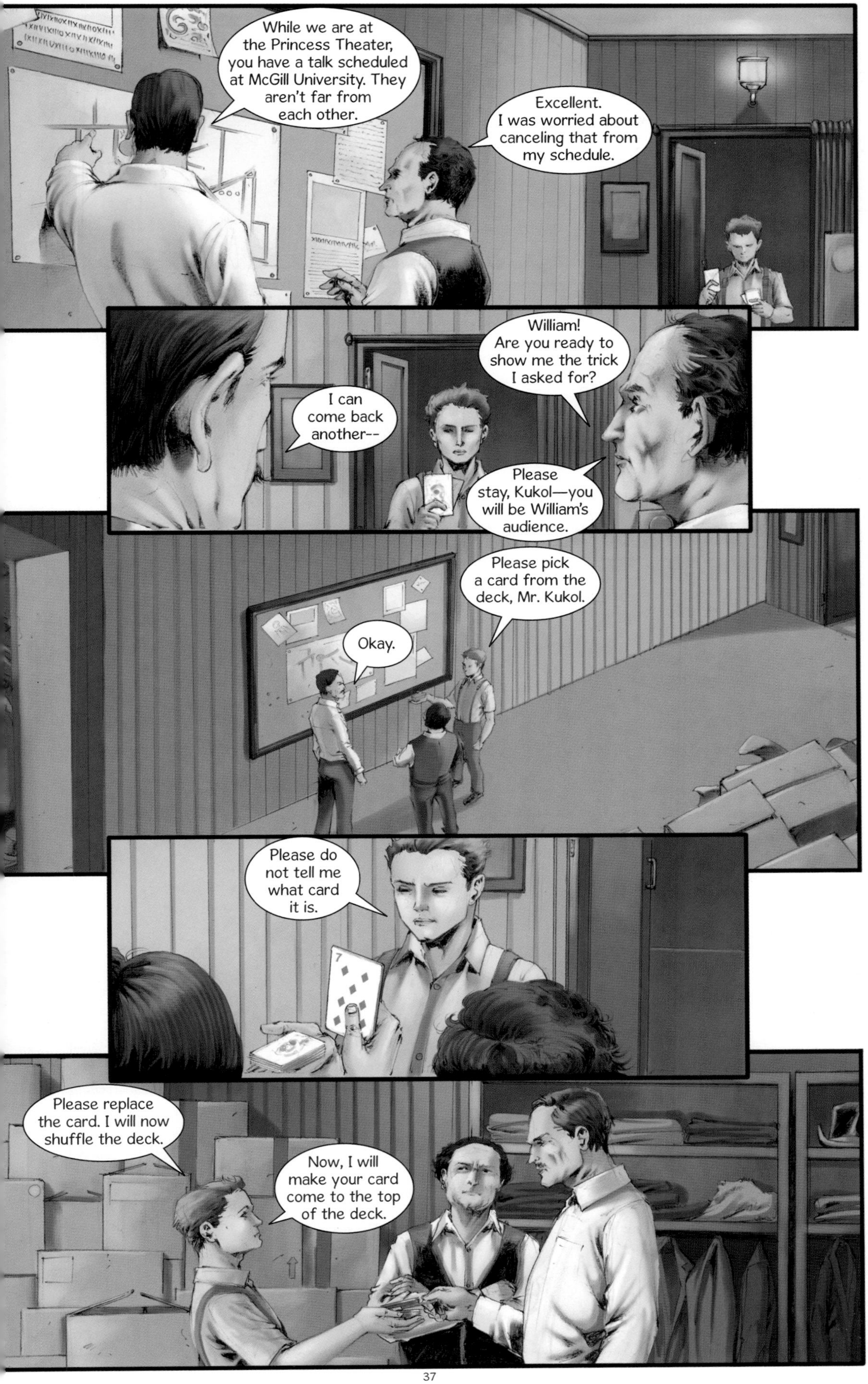
While we are at the Princess Theater, you have a talk scheduled at McGill University. They aren't far from each other.
Excellent. I was worried about canceling that from my schedule.
William! Are you ready to show me the trick I asked for?
I can come back another--
Please stay, Kukol—you will be William's audience.
Please pick a card from the deck, Mr. Kukol.
Okay.
Please do not tell me what card it is.
Please replace the card. I will now shuffle the deck.
Now, I will make your card come to the top of the deck.

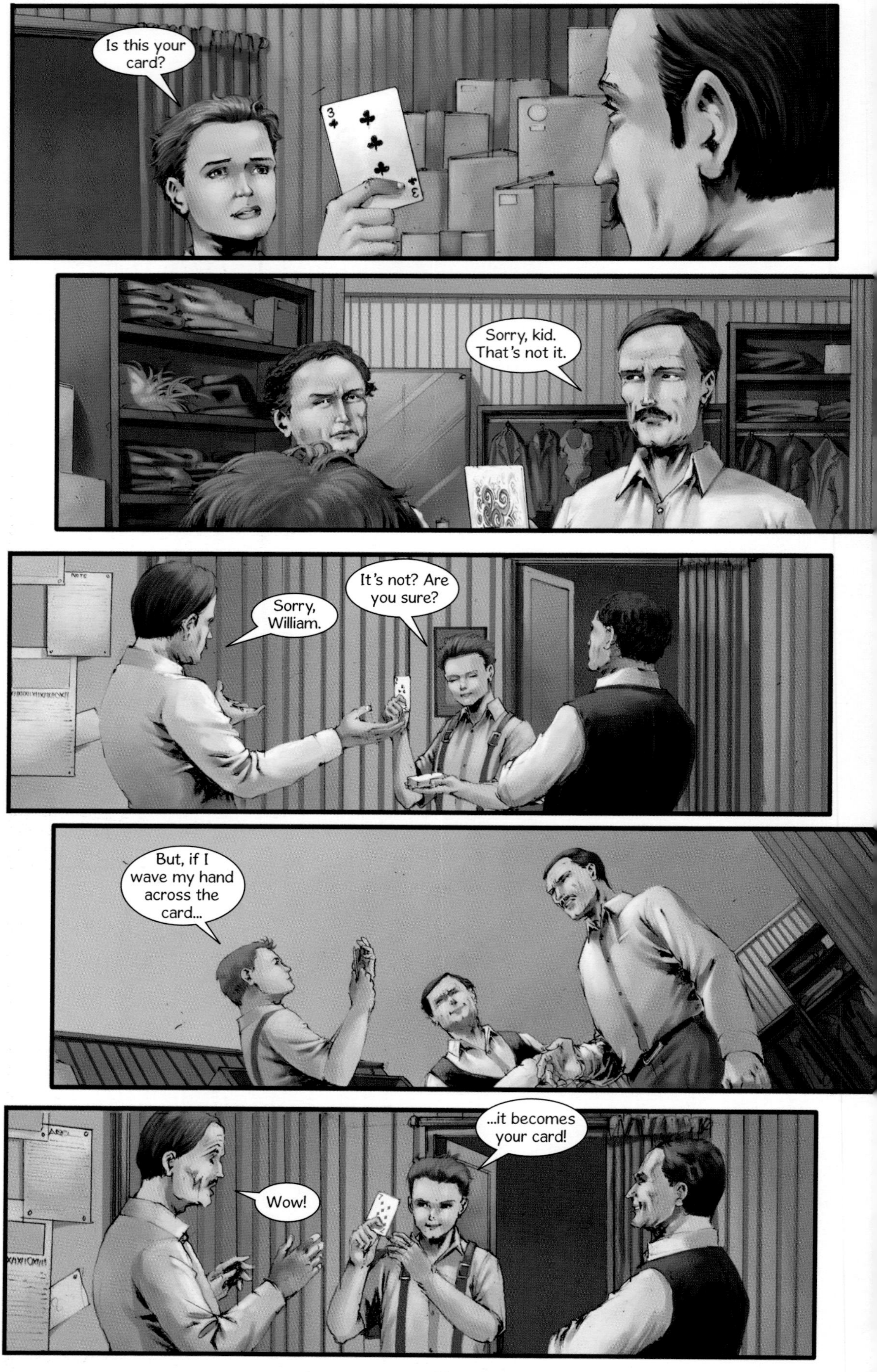
Is this your card?
Sorry, kid. That's not it.
Sorry, William.
It's not? Are you sure?
But, if I wave my hand across the card...
...it becomes your card!
Wow!

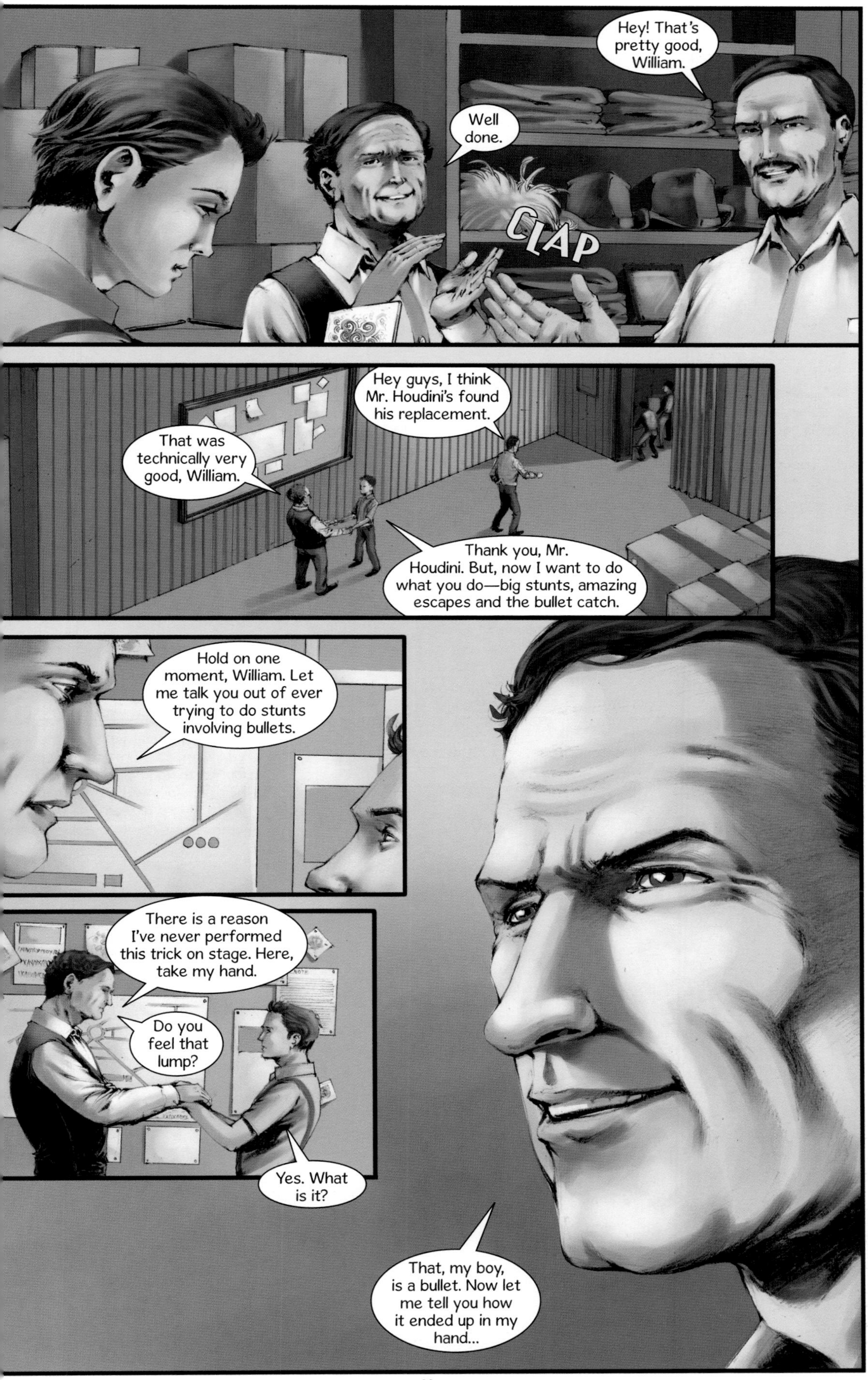
Well done.
Hey! That's pretty good, William.
CLAP
That was technically very good, William.
Hey guys, I think Mr. Houdini's found his replacement.
Thank you, Mr. Houdini. But, now I want to do what you do—big stunts, amazing escapes and the bullet catch.
Hold on one moment, William. Let me talk you out of ever trying to do stunts involving bullets.
There is a reason I've never performed this trick on stage. Here, take my hand.
Do you feel that lump?
Yes. What is it?
That, my boy, is a bullet. Now let me tell you how it ended up in my hand...

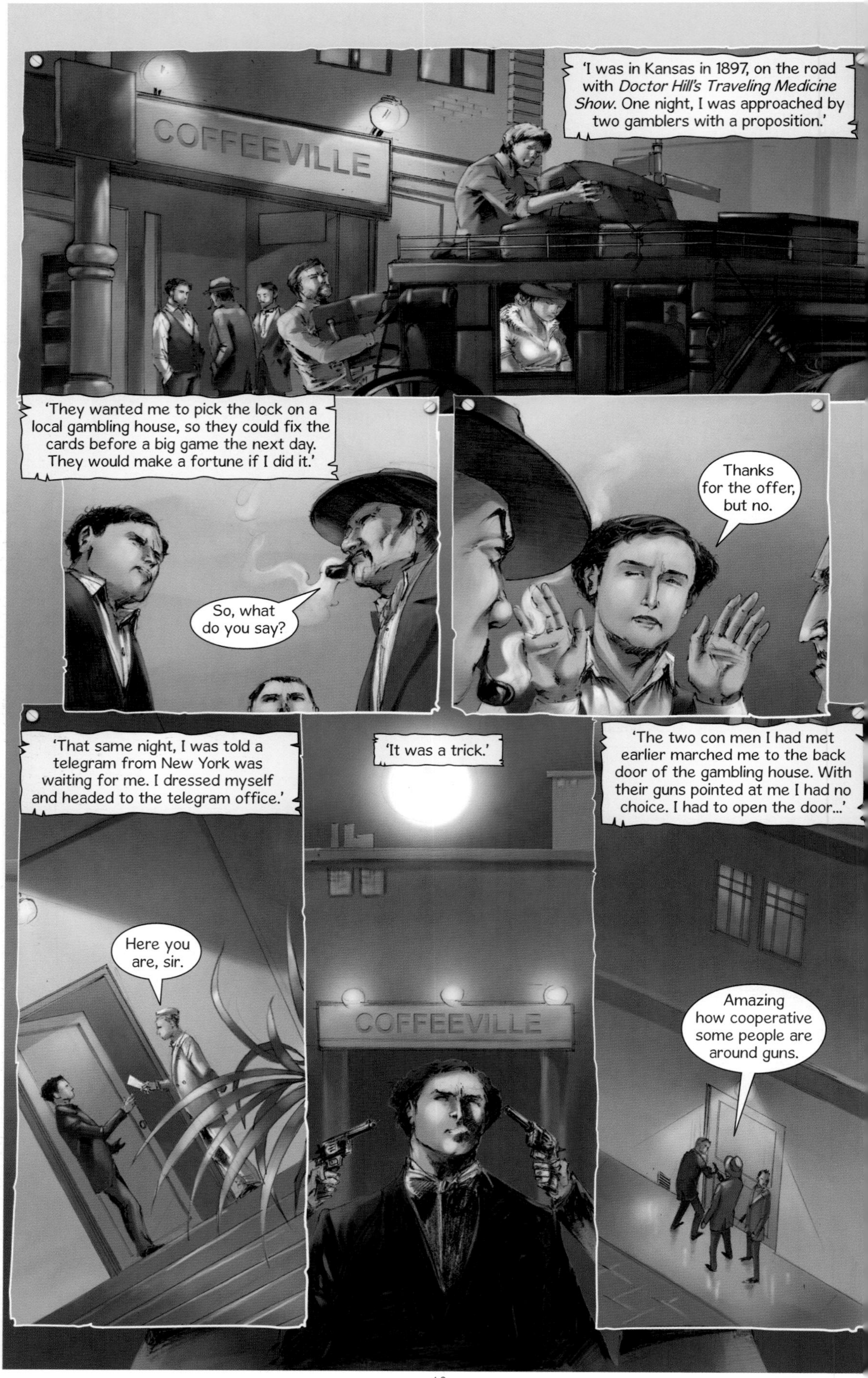
'I was in Kansas in 1897, on the road with *Doctor Hill's Traveling Medicine Show*. One night, I was approached by two gamblers with a proposition.'
COFFEEVILLE
'They wanted me to pick the lock on a local gambling house, so they could fix the cards before a big game the next day. They would make a fortune if I did it.'
So, what do you say?
Thanks for the offer, but no.
'That same night, I was told a telegram from New York was waiting for me. I dressed myself and headed to the telegram office.'
Here you are, sir.
'It was a trick.'
COFFEEVILLE
'The two con men I had met earlier marched me to the back door of the gambling house. With their guns pointed at me I had no choice. I had to open the door...'
Amazing how cooperative some people are around guns.

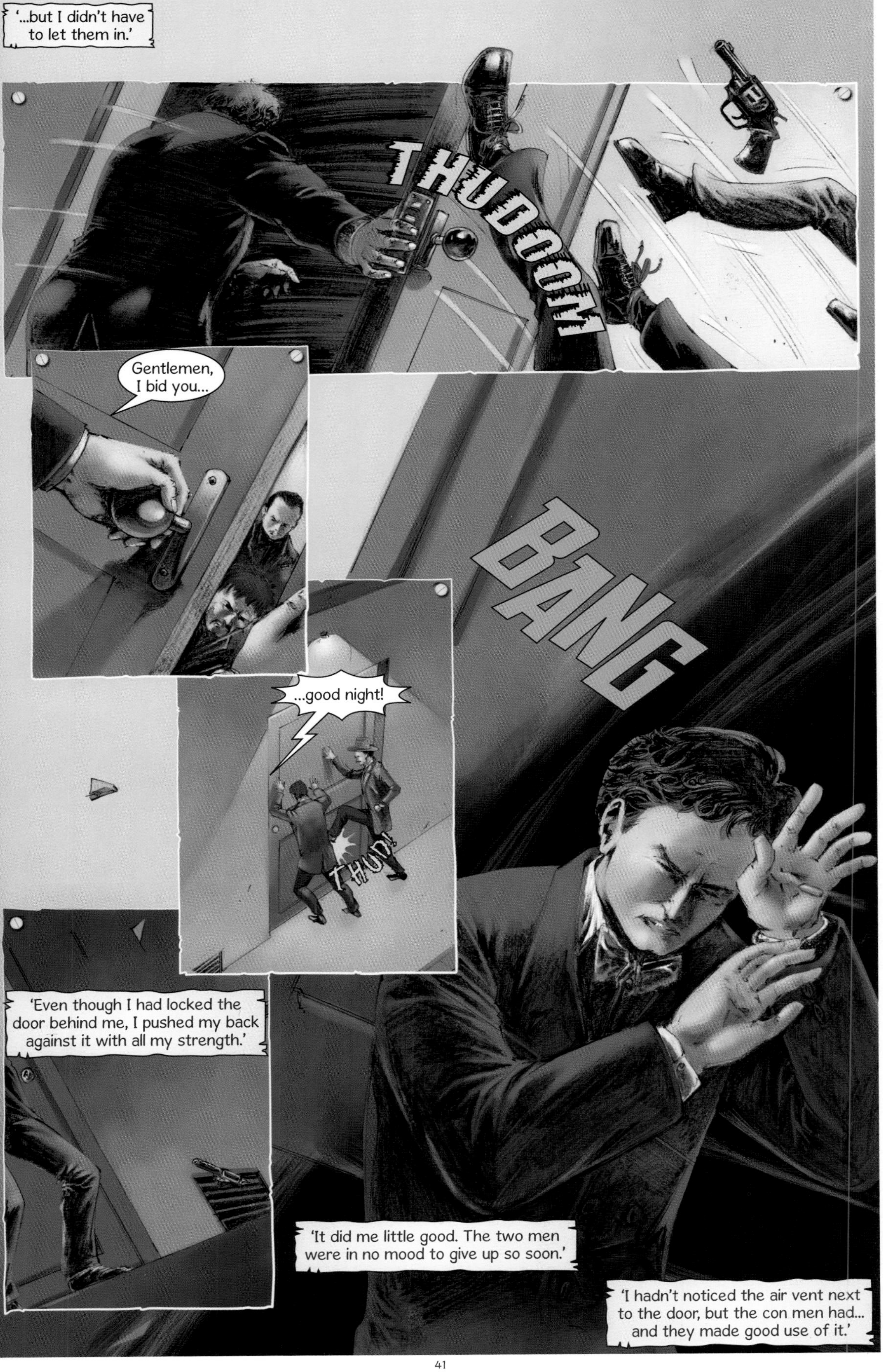
'...but I didn't have to let them in.'
THUDOOM
Gentlemen, I bid you...
BANG
...good night!
THUD!
'Even though I had locked the door behind me, I pushed my back against it with all my strength.'
'It did me little good. The two men were in no mood to give up so soon.'
'I hadn't noticed the air vent next to the door, but the con men had... and they made good use of it.'

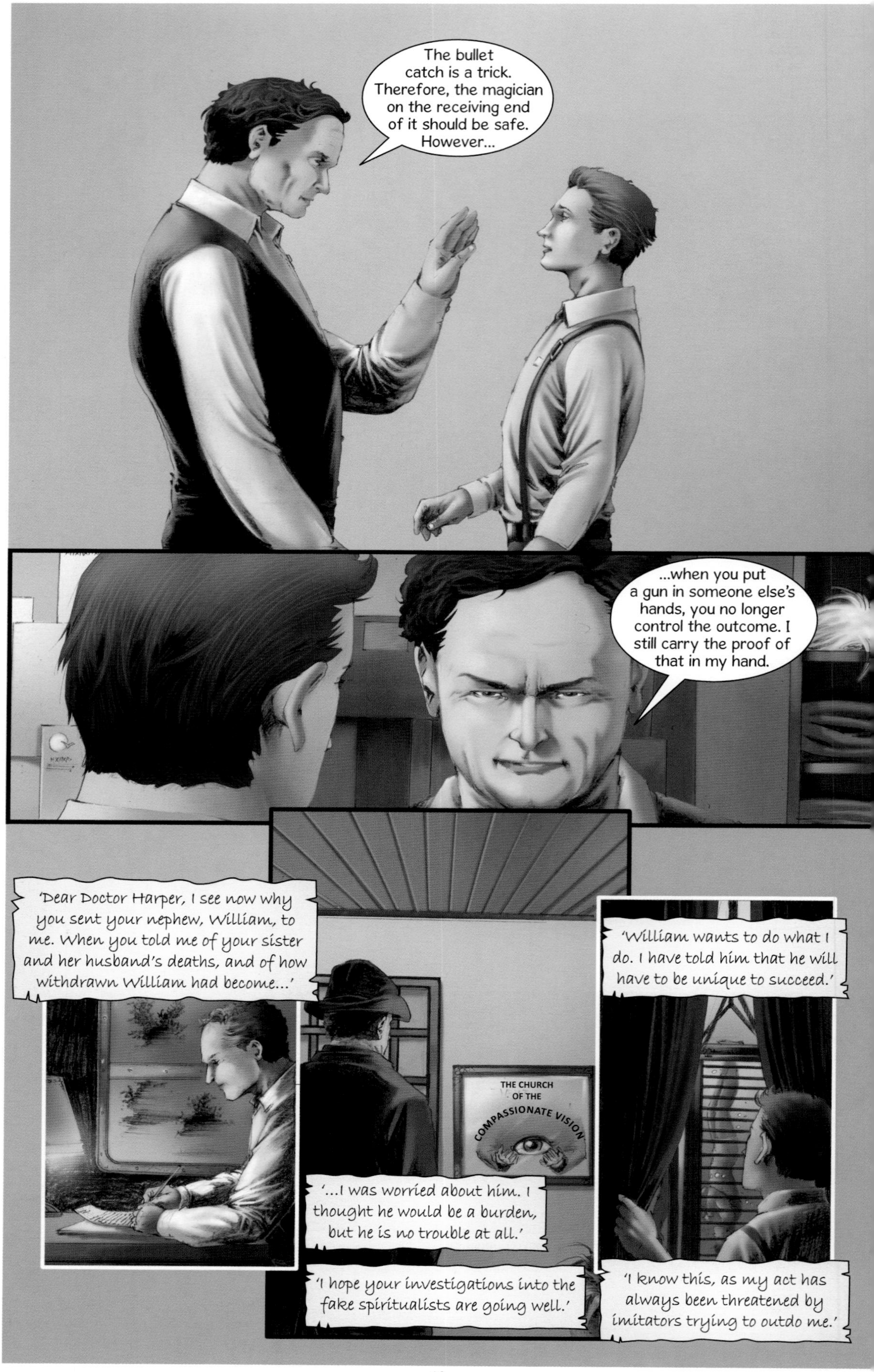
The bullet catch is a trick. Therefore, the magician on the receiving end of it should be safe. However...
...when you put a gun in someone else's hands, you no longer control the outcome. I still carry the proof of that in my hand.
'Dear Doctor Harper, I see now why you sent your nephew, William, to me. When you told me of your sister and her husband's deaths, and of how withdrawn William had become...'
'...I was worried about him. I thought he would be a burden, but he is no trouble at all.'
THE CHURCH OF THE COMPASSIONATE VISION
'I hope your investigations into the fake spiritualists are going well.'
'William wants to do what I do. I have told him that he will have to be unique to succeed.'
'I know this, as my act has always been threatened by imitators trying to outdo me.'

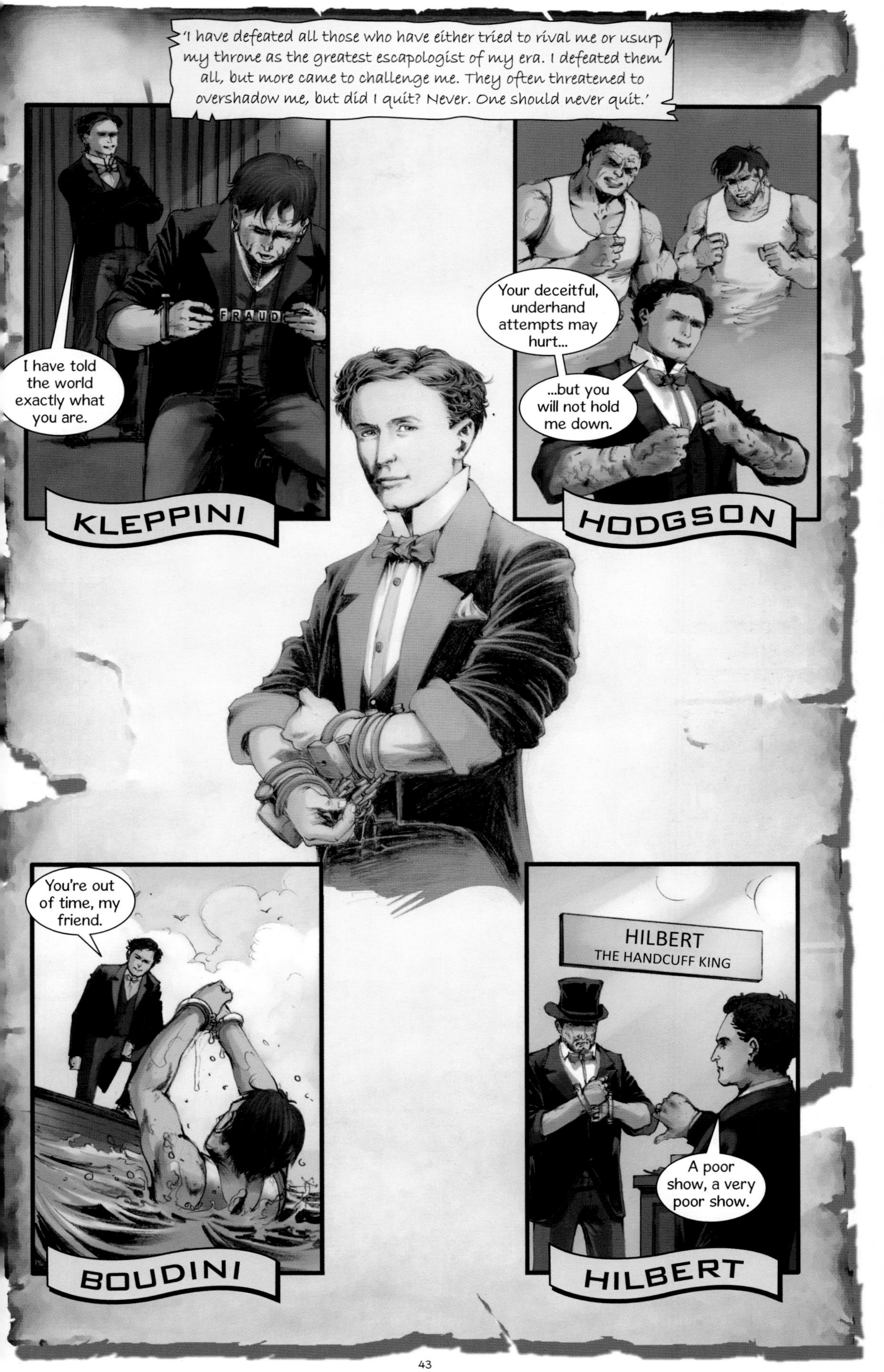
'I have defeated all those who have either tried to rival me or usurp my throne as the greatest escapologist of my era. I defeated them all, but more came to challenge me. They often threatened to overshadow me, but did I quit? Never. One should never quit.'
FRAUD
I have told the world exactly what you are.
KLEPPINI
Your deceitful, underhand attempts may hurt...
...but you will not hold me down.
HODGSON
You're out of time, my friend.
BOUDINI
HILBERT
THE HANDCUFF KING
A poor show, a very poor show.
HILBERT

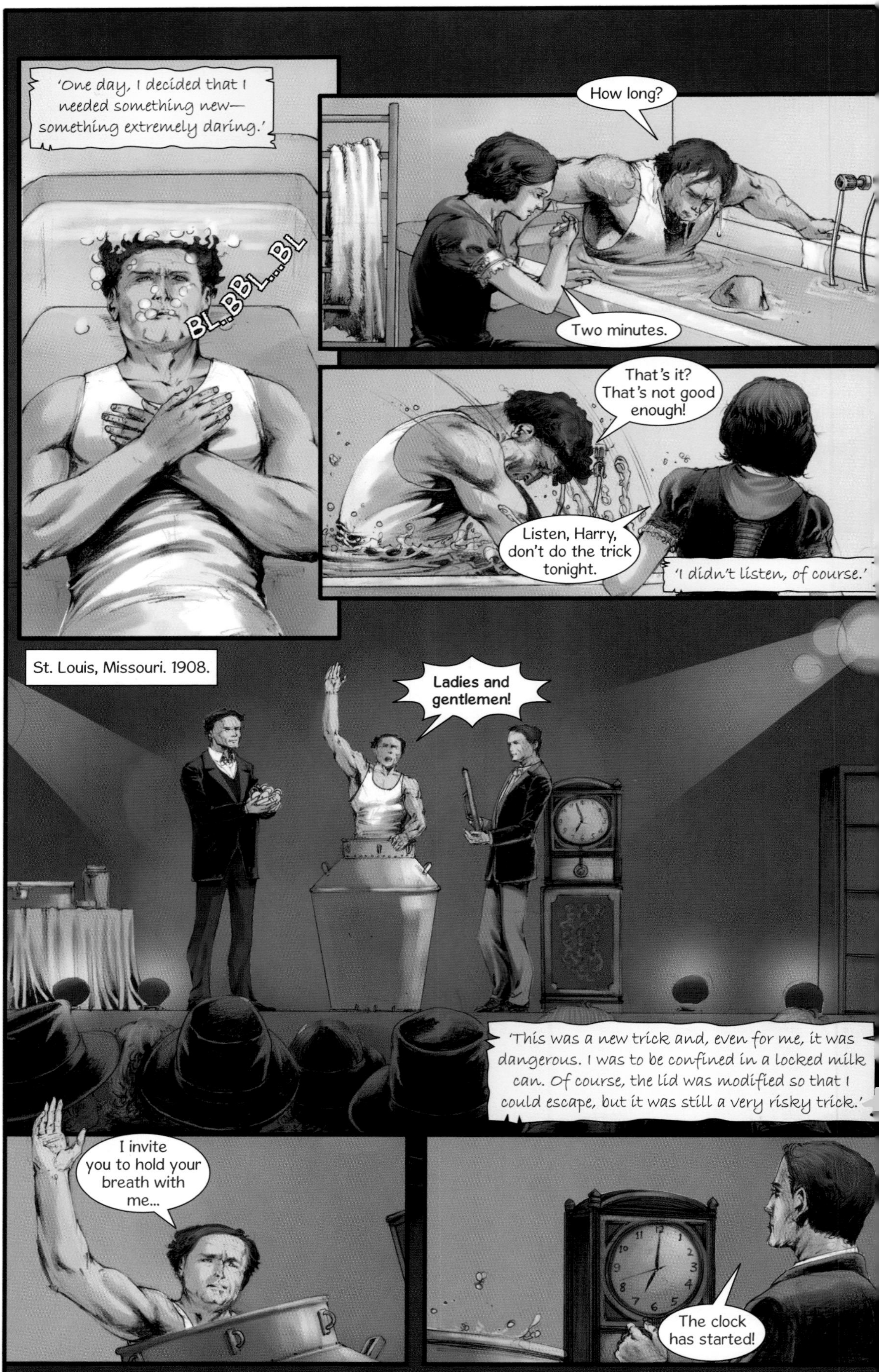
'One day, I decided that I needed something new—something extremely daring.'
BL..BBL...BL
How long?
Two minutes.
That's it? That's not good enough!
Listen, Harry, don't do the trick tonight.
'I didn't listen, of course.'
St. Louis, Missouri. 1908.
Ladies and gentlemen!
'This was a new trick and, even for me, it was dangerous. I was to be confined in a locked milk can. Of course, the lid was modified so that I could escape, but it was still a very risky trick.'
I invite you to hold your breath with me...
The clock has started!

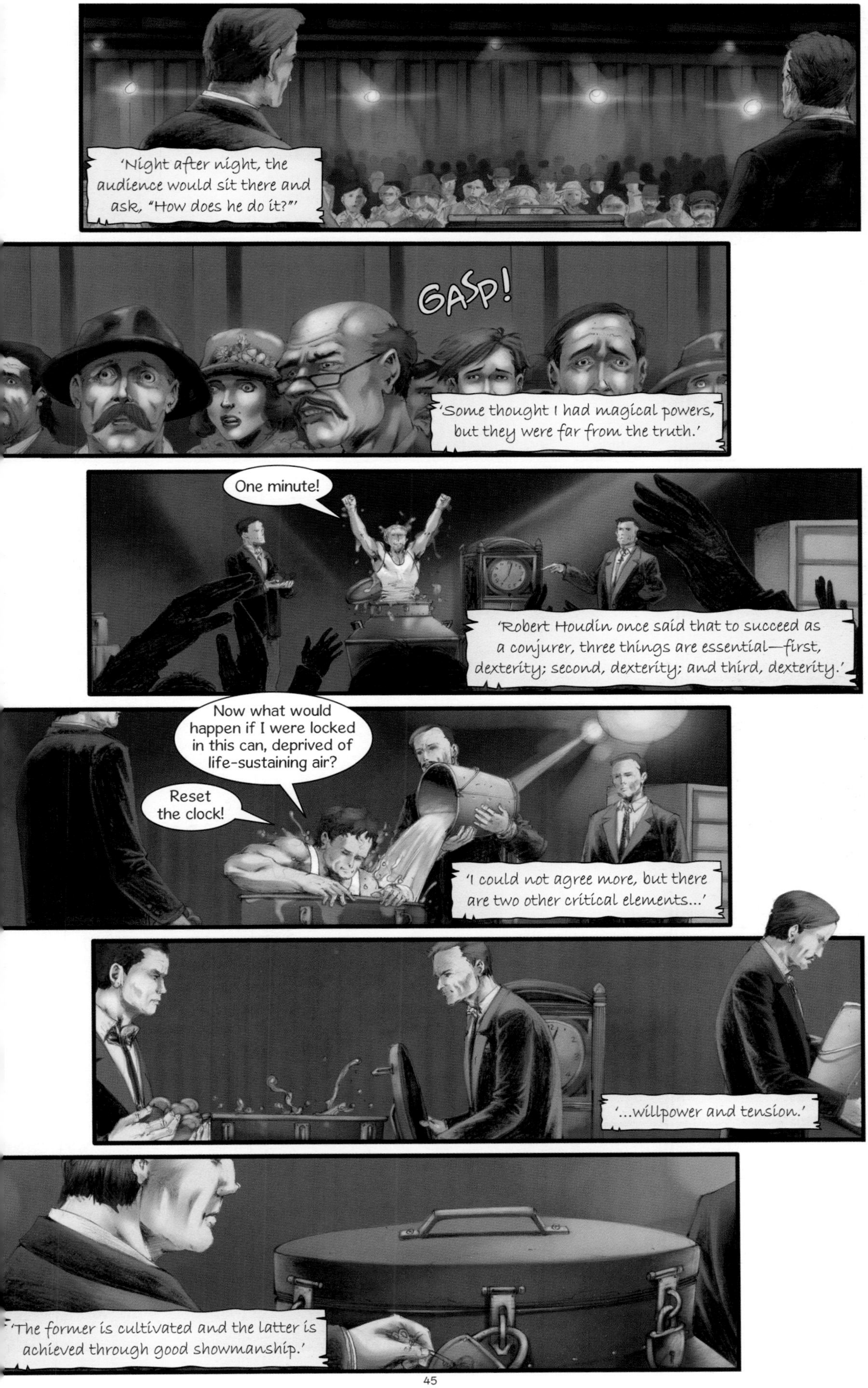
'Night after night, the audience would sit there and ask, "How does he do it?"'
GASP!
'Some thought I had magical powers, but they were far from the truth.'
One minute!
'Robert Houdin once said that to succeed as a conjurer, three things are essential—first, dexterity; second, dexterity; and third, dexterity.'
Now what would happen if I were locked in this can, deprived of life-sustaining air?
Reset the clock!
'I could not agree more, but there are two other critical elements...'
'...willpower and tension.'
'The former is cultivated and the latter is achieved through good showmanship.'

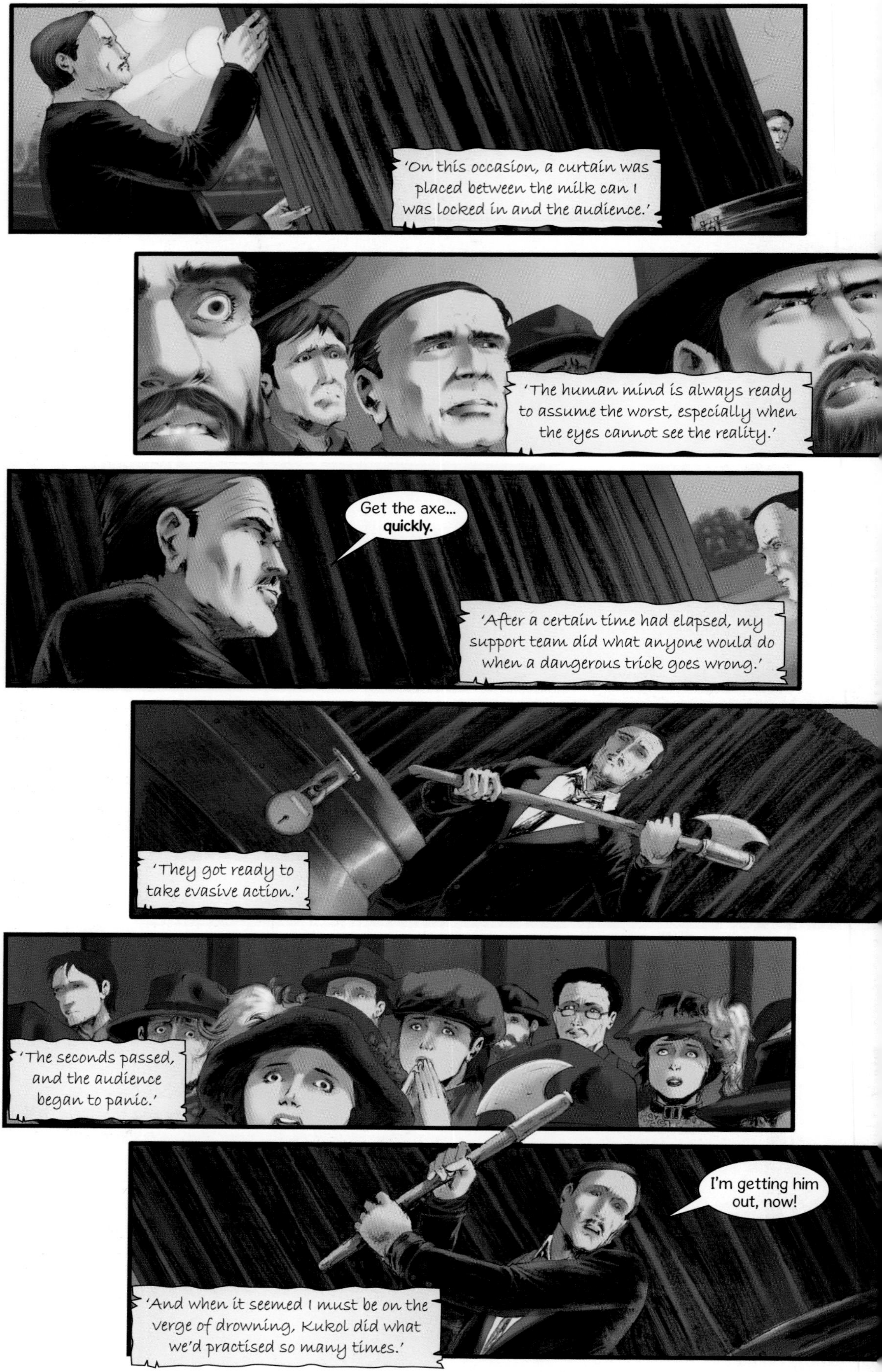
'On this occasion, a curtain was placed between the milk can I was locked in and the audience.'
'The human mind is always ready to assume the worst, especially when the eyes cannot see the reality.'
Get the axe... **quickly.**
'After a certain time had elapsed, my support team did what anyone would do when a dangerous trick goes wrong.'
'They got ready to take evasive action.'
'The seconds passed, and the audience began to panic.'
I'm getting him out, now!
'And when it seemed I must be on the verge of drowning, Kukol did what we'd practised so many times.'

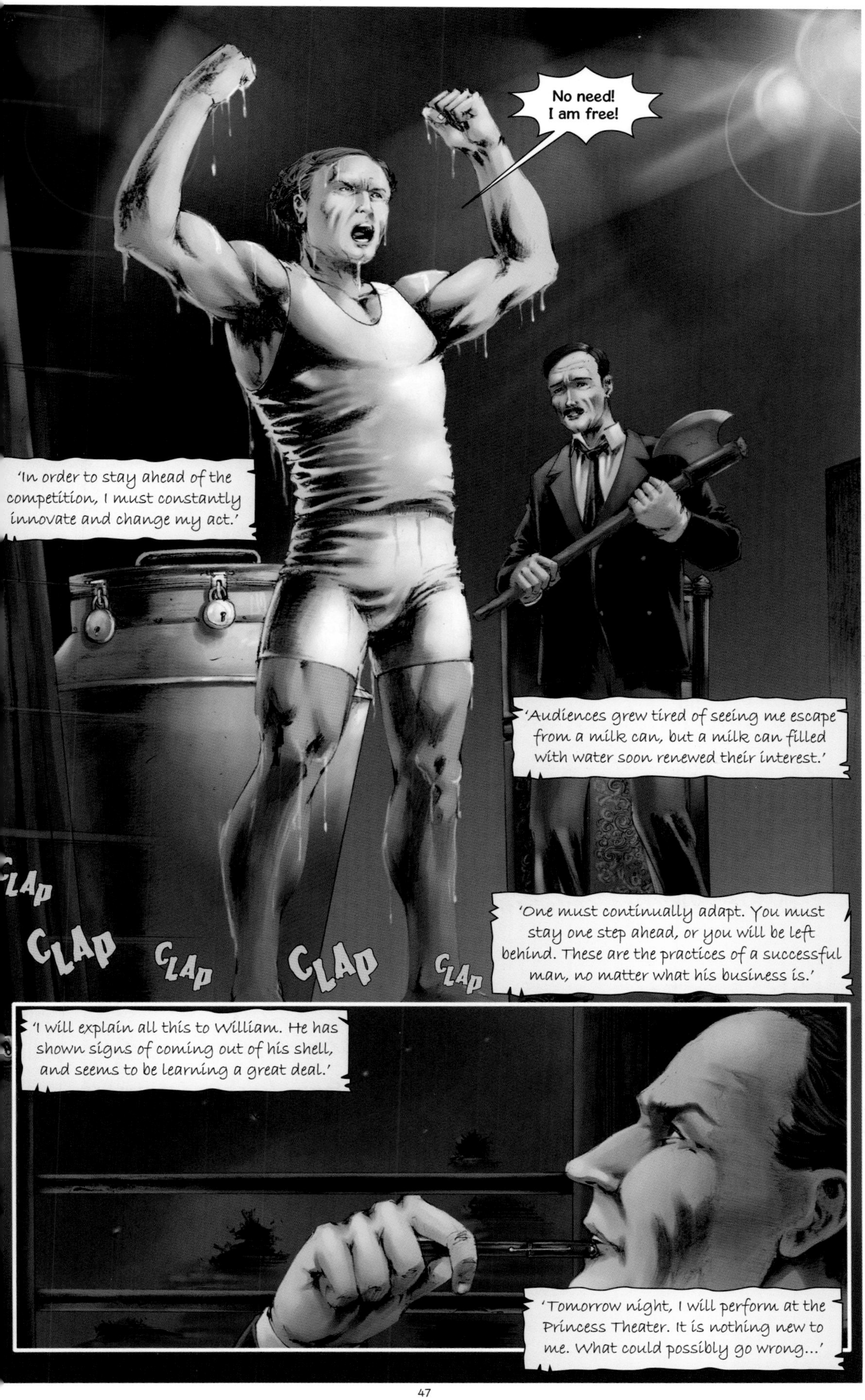
No need! I am free!
'In order to stay ahead of the competition, I must constantly innovate and change my act.'
'Audiences grew tired of seeing me escape from a milk can, but a milk can filled with water soon renewed their interest.'
CLAP CLAP CLAP CLAP CLAP
'One must continually adapt. You must stay one step ahead, or you will be left behind. These are the practices of a successful man, no matter what his business is.'
'I will explain all this to William. He has shown signs of coming out of his shell, and seems to be learning a great deal.'
'Tomorrow night, I will perform at the Princess Theater. It is nothing new to me. What could possibly go wrong...'

October 21, 1926

I have found, in trying to write a biography, that locating information about someone's childhood is the most difficult of tasks. Many of the people that Houdini grew up with have died, others are difficult to track down, and some have left the country.

From visiting his old school, and speaking to people who lived in his old neighborhood, I have found out that Houdini has had a lifelong obsession with physical fitness.

While at school, he won awards for his track and field achievements. It is also rumored that Houdini would often go out running, sometimes for ten miles at a stretch!

His dedication as a swimmer at a young age puts an end to the rumor that he has a fear of water. It is said that he has had to overcome that fear to perform his underwater escapes. This is obviously untrue.

Houdini's height is five foot six and, it seems, he decided that his small stature would benefit from bodybuilding. He seems to have used many methods to develop his physique and, when you meet him in person, the first thing you will notice is his thickset body and strong arms.

Of course, it is obvious from the physical nature of his work that his dexterity must be honed to perfection. One need only look at his escapes from a straitjacket, while suspended upside down. Heaven only knows what strain that places on his spine, as he wriggles back and forth so forcefully, in an attempt to free himself.

Eventually, it seems, all famous people become legends based on rumors and conflicting accounts. Houdini, although still alive, seems to be no different to that rule.

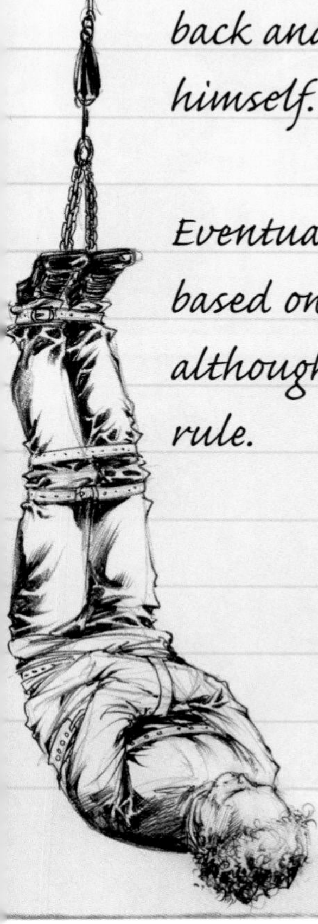

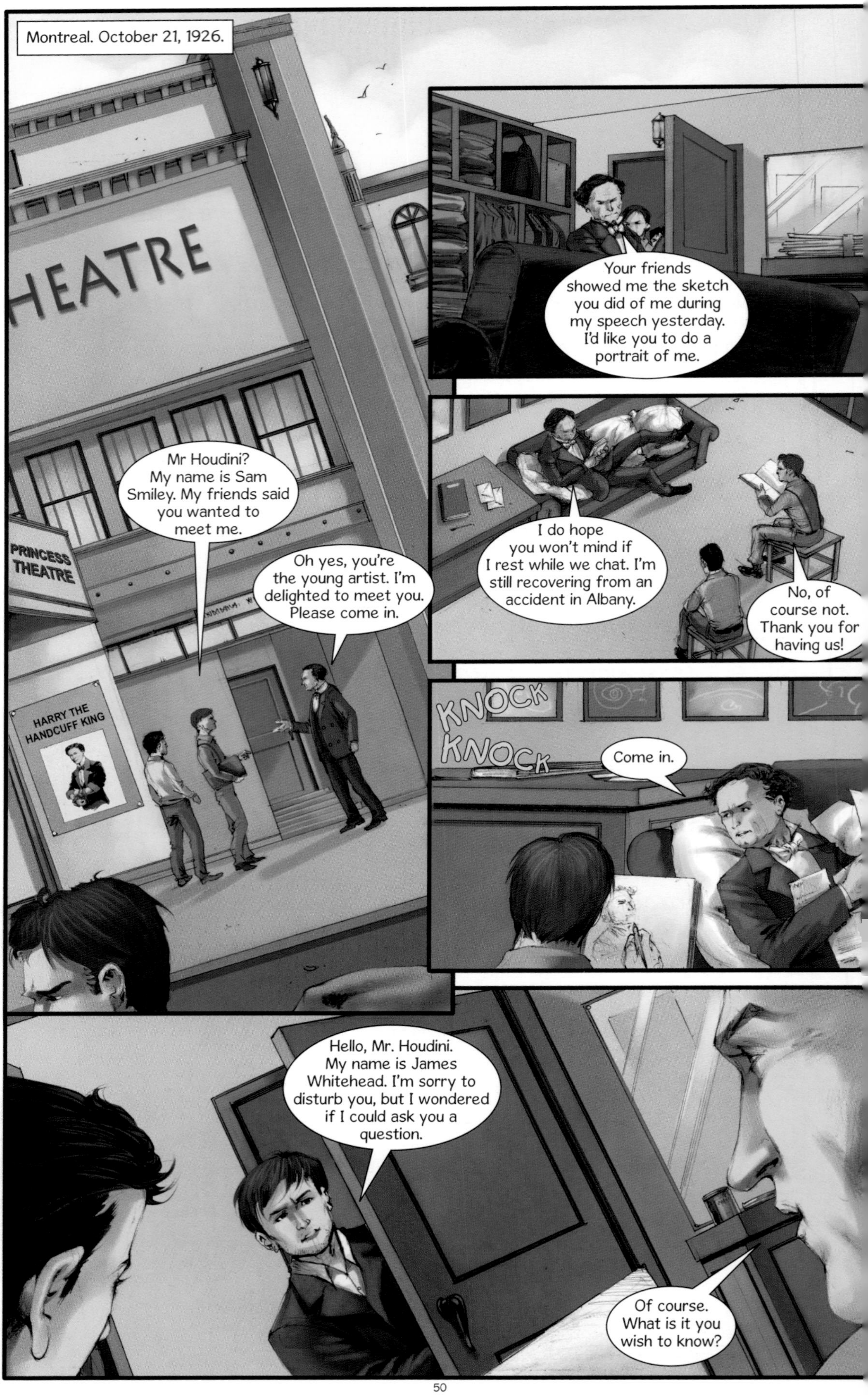

Montreal. October 21, 1926.
THEATRE
PRINCESS THEATRE
HARRY THE HANDCUFF KING
Mr Houdini? My name is Sam Smiley. My friends said you wanted to meet me.
Oh yes, you're the young artist. I'm delighted to meet you. Please come in.
Your friends showed me the sketch you did of me during my speech yesterday. I'd like you to do a portrait of me.
I do hope you won't mind if I rest while we chat. I'm still recovering from an accident in Albany.
No, of course not. Thank you for having us!
KNOCK KNOCK
Come in.
Hello, Mr. Houdini. My name is James Whitehead. I'm sorry to disturb you, but I wondered if I could ask you a question.
Of course. What is it you wish to know?

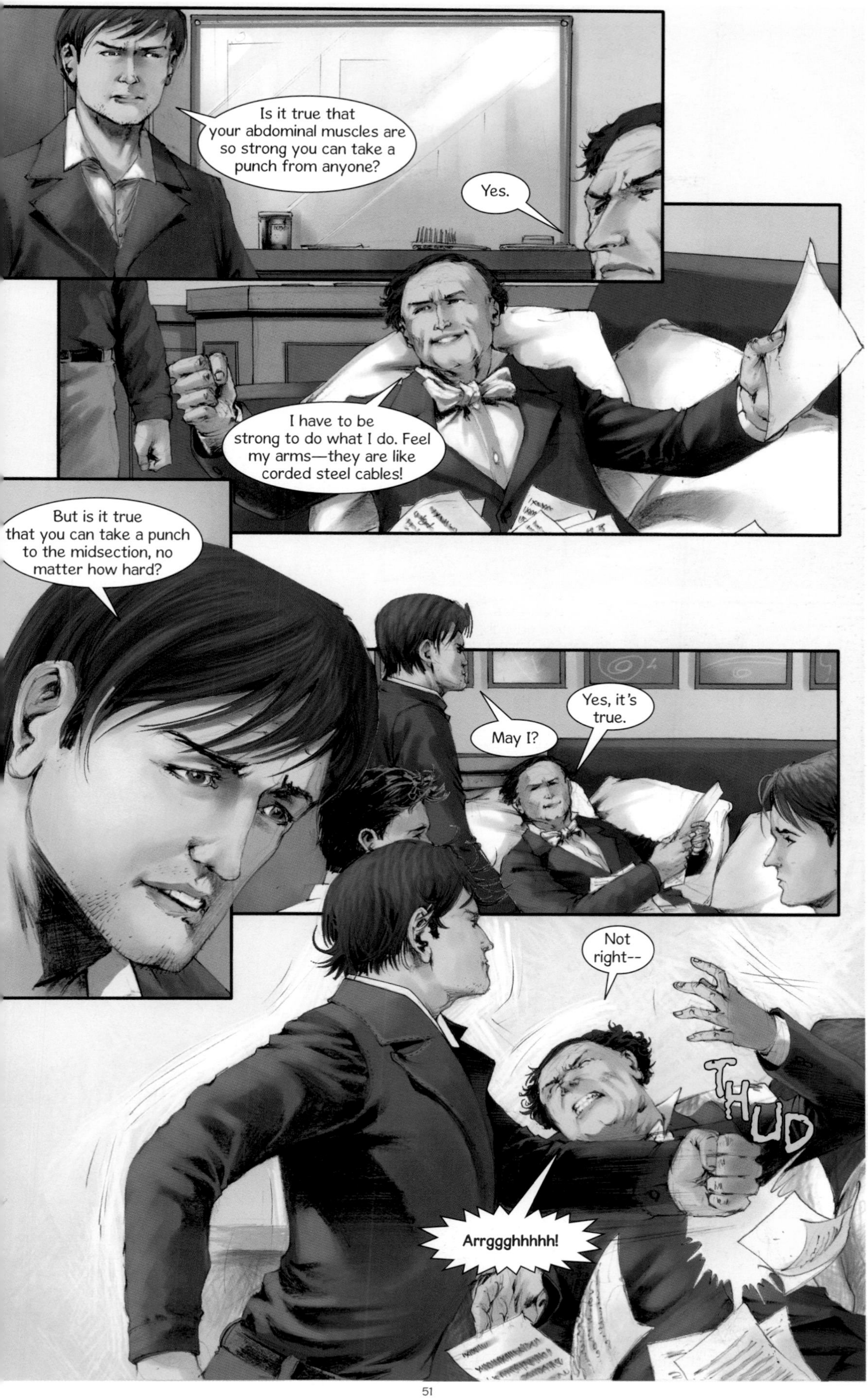
Is it true that your abdominal muscles are so strong you can take a punch from anyone?
Yes.
I have to be strong to do what I do. Feel my arms—they are like corded steel cables!
But is it true that you can take a punch to the midsection, no matter how hard?
May I?
Yes, it's true.
Not right--
THUD
Arrggghhhhh!

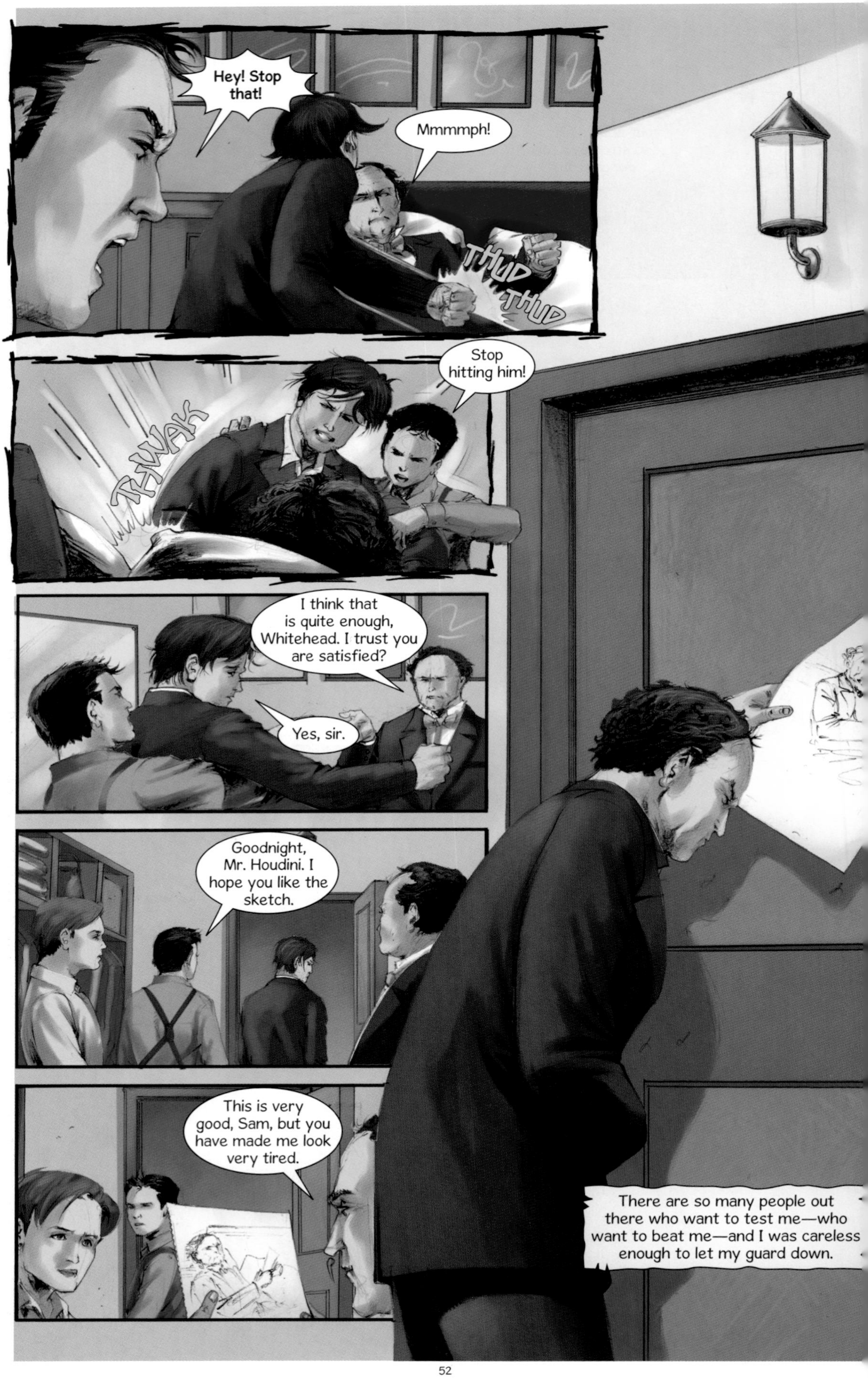
Hey! Stop that!
Mmmmph!
THUD THUD
Stop hitting him!
THWAK
I think that is quite enough, Whitehead. I trust you are satisfied?
Yes, sir.
Goodnight, Mr. Houdini. I hope you like the sketch.
This is very good, Sam, but you have made me look very tired.
There are so many people out there who want to test me—who want to beat me—and I was careless enough to let my guard down.

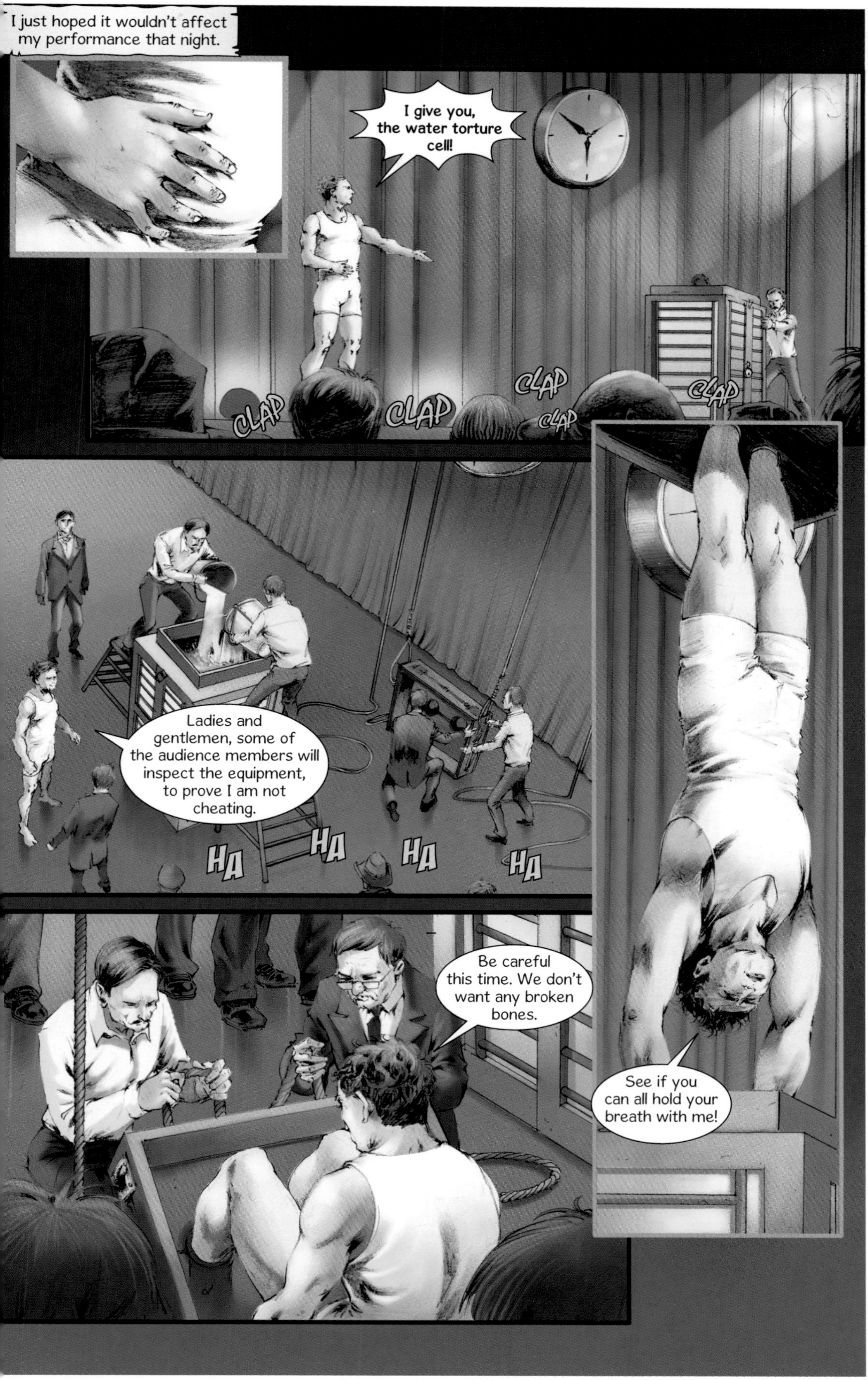
I just hoped it wouldn't affect my performance that night.
I give you, the water torture cell!
CLAP CLAP CLAP CLAP CLAP
Ladies and gentlemen, some of the audience members will inspect the equipment, to prove I am not cheating.
HA HA HA HA
Be careful this time. We don't want any broken bones.
See if you can all hold your breath with me!

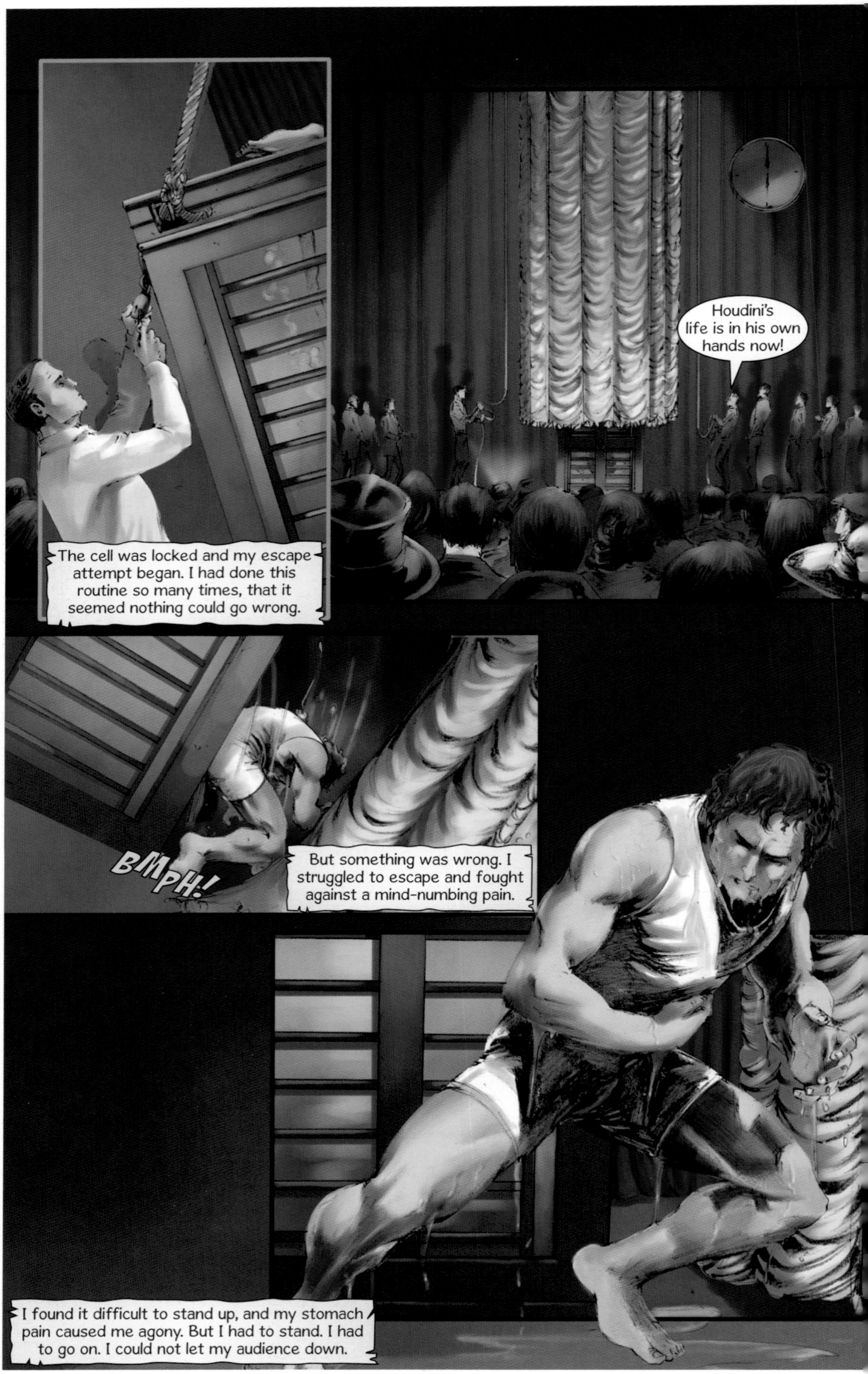
The cell was locked and my escape attempt began. I had done this routine so many times, that it seemed nothing could go wrong.
Houdini's life is in his own hands now!
BMPH!
But something was wrong. I struggled to escape and fought against a mind-numbing pain.
I found it difficult to stand up, and my stomach pain caused me agony. But I had to stand. I had to go on. I could not let my audience down.

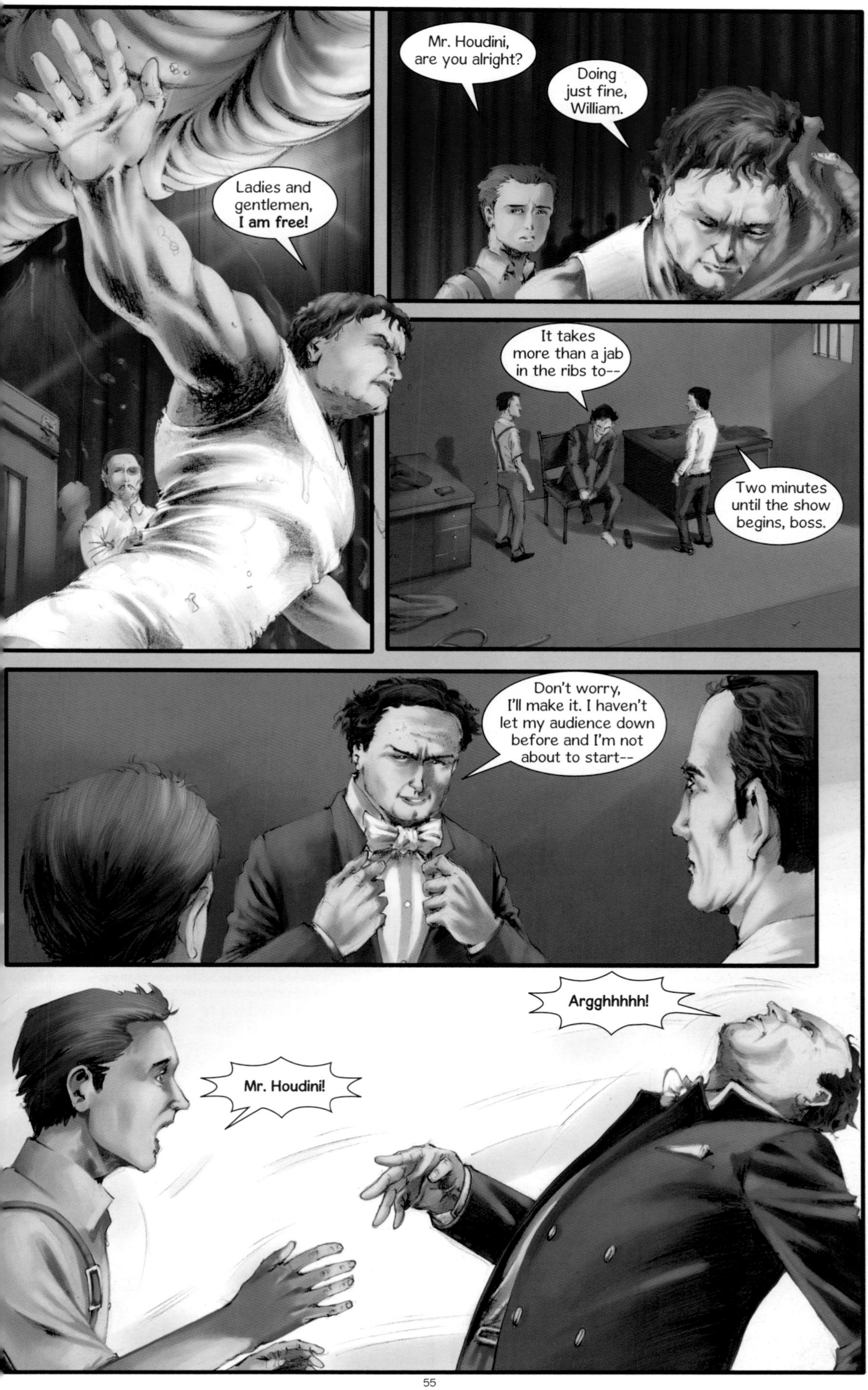
Ladies and gentlemen, **I am free!**
Mr. Houdini, are you alright?
Doing just fine, William.
It takes more than a jab in the ribs to--
Two minutes until the show begins, boss.
Don't worry, I'll make it. I haven't let my audience down before and I'm not about to start--
Argghhhhh!
Mr. Houdini!

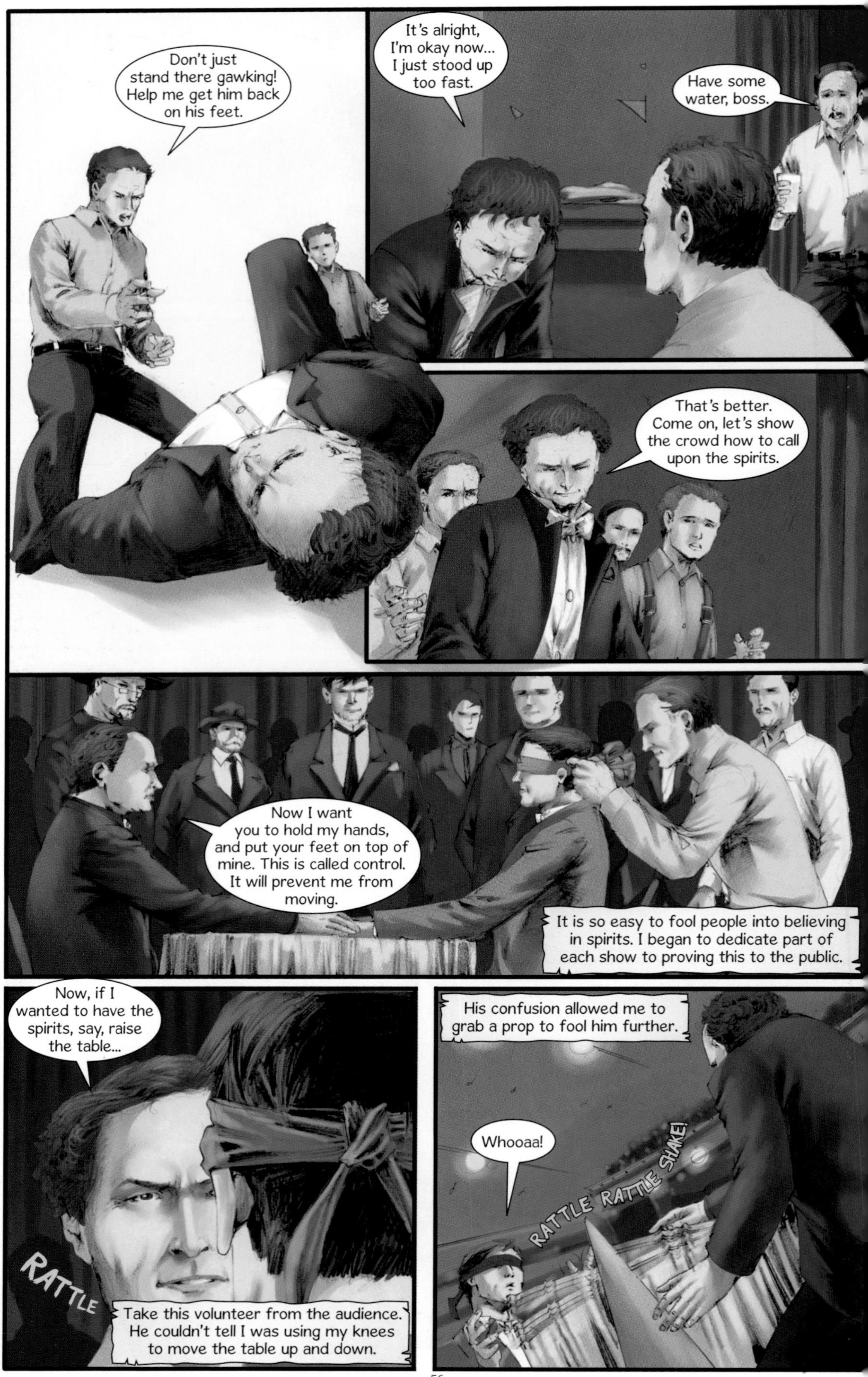
Don't just stand there gawking! Help me get him back on his feet.
It's alright, I'm okay now... I just stood up too fast.
Have some water, boss.
That's better. Come on, let's show the crowd how to call upon the spirits.
Now I want you to hold my hands, and put your feet on top of mine. This is called control. It will prevent me from moving.
It is so easy to fool people into believing in spirits. I began to dedicate part of each show to proving this to the public.
Now, if I wanted to have the spirits, say, raise the table...
RATTLE
Take this volunteer from the audience. He couldn't tell I was using my knees to move the table up and down.
His confusion allowed me to grab a prop to fool him further.
Whooaa!
RATTLE RATTLE SHAKE!

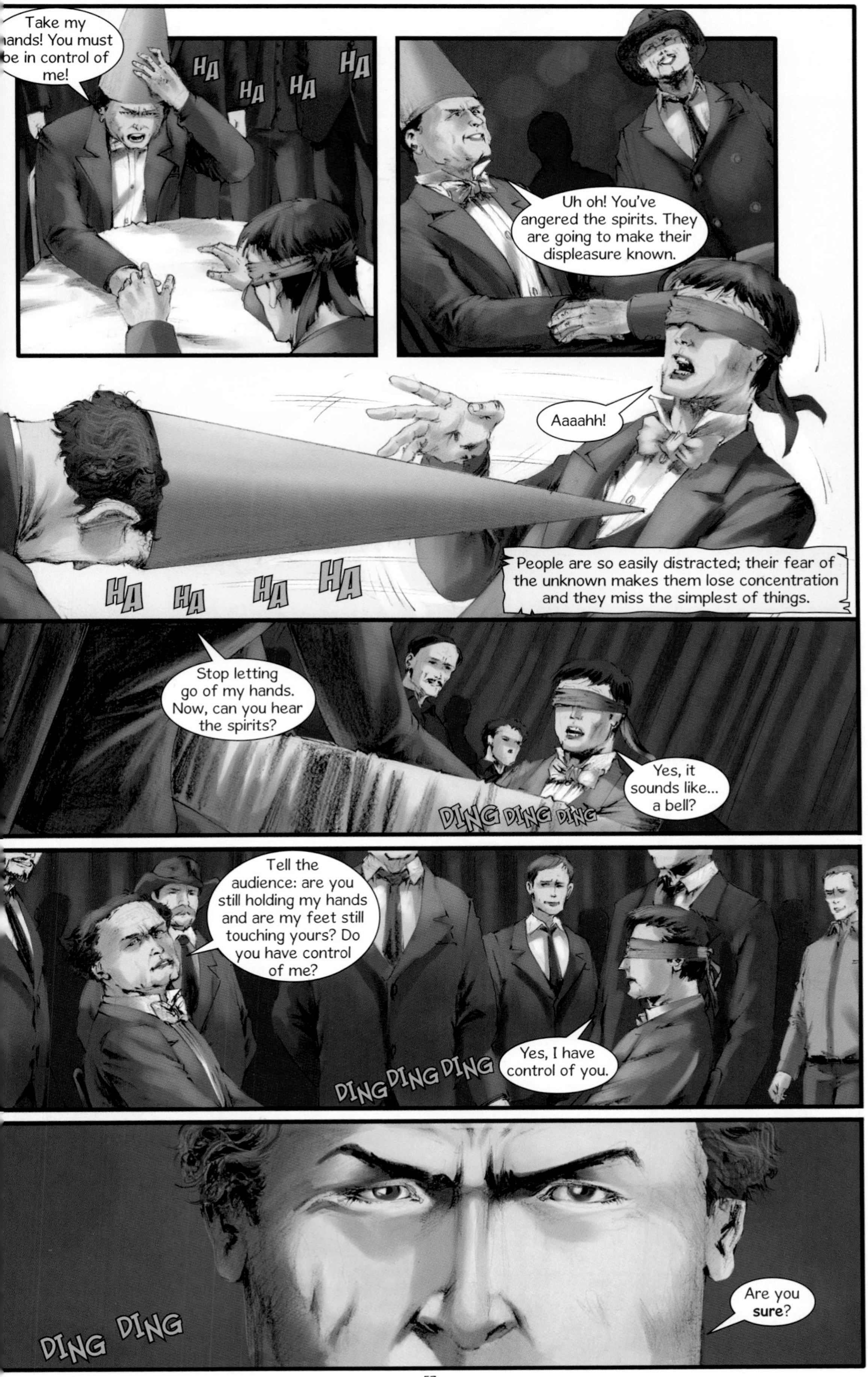
Take my hands! You must be in control of me!
HA HA HA HA
Uh oh! You've angered the spirits. They are going to make their displeasure known.
Aaaahh!
HA HA HA HA
People are so easily distracted; their fear of the unknown makes them lose concentration and they miss the simplest of things.
Stop letting go of my hands. Now, can you hear the spirits?
Yes, it sounds like... a bell?
DING DING DING
Tell the audience: are you still holding my hands and are my feet still touching yours? Do you have control of me?
Yes, I have control of you.
DING DING DING
DING DING
Are you **sure**?

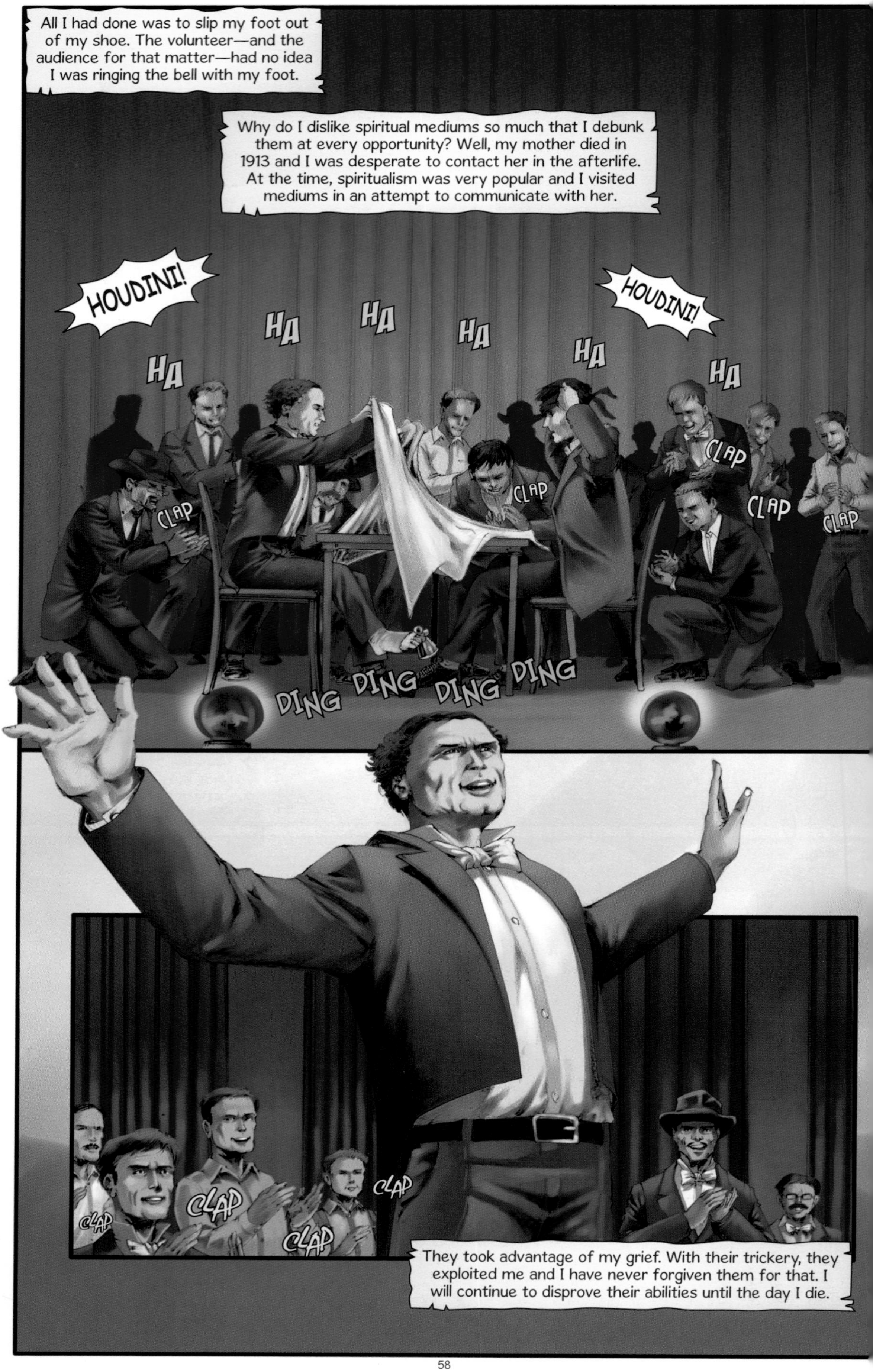
All I had done was to slip my foot out of my shoe. The volunteer—and the audience for that matter—had no idea I was ringing the bell with my foot.
Why do I dislike spiritual mediums so much that I debunk them at every opportunity? Well, my mother died in 1913 and I was desperate to contact her in the afterlife. At the time, spiritualism was very popular and I visited mediums in an attempt to communicate with her.
HOUDINI!
HOUDINI!
HA HA HA HA HA HA
CLAP CLAP CLAP CLAP CLAP
DING DING DING DING
CLAP CLAP CLAP CLAP
They took advantage of my grief. With their trickery, they exploited me and I have never forgiven them for that. I will continue to disprove their abilities until the day I die.

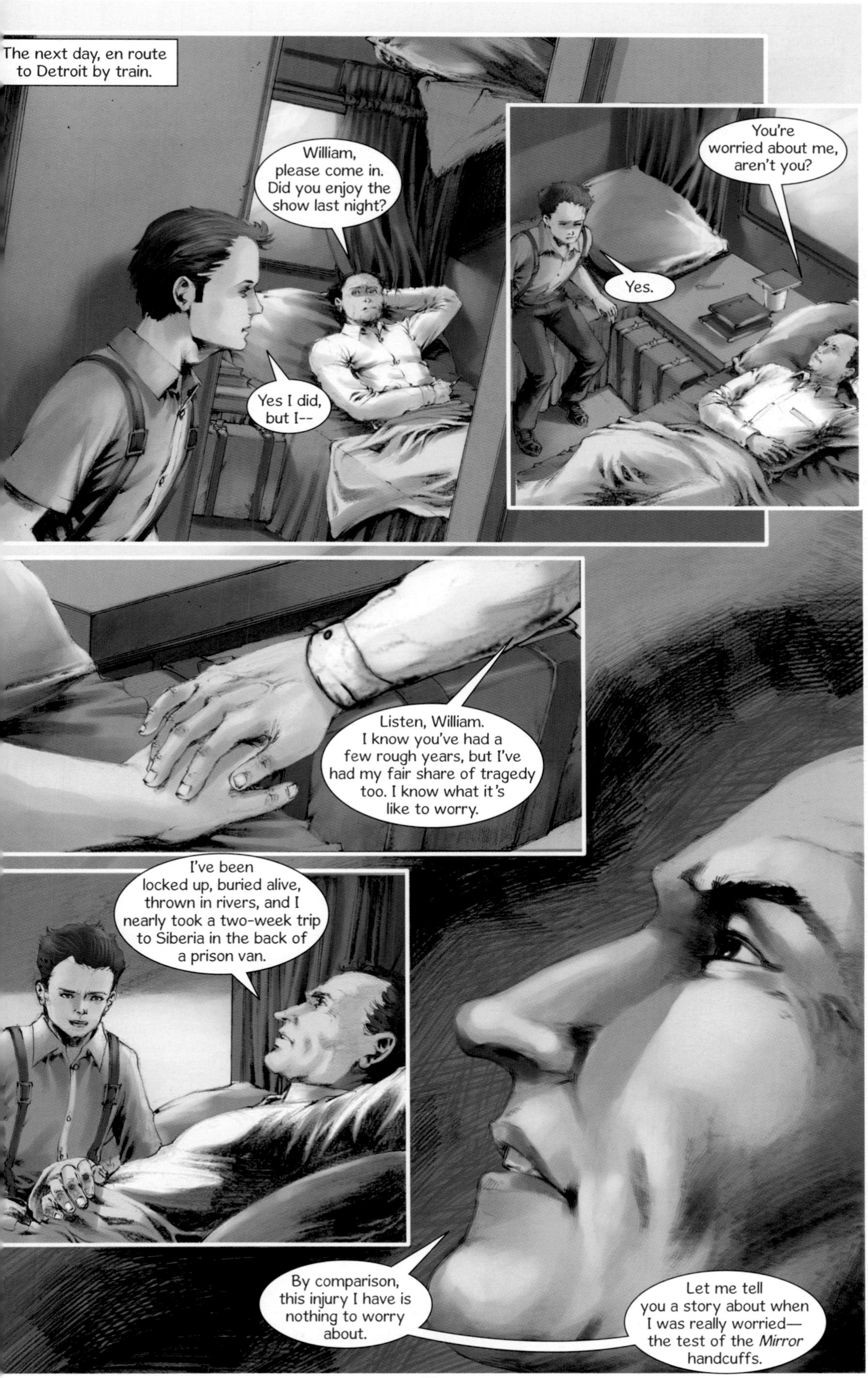
The next day, en route to Detroit by train.
William, please come in. Did you enjoy the show last night?
Yes I did, but I--
You're worried about me, aren't you?
Yes.
Listen, William. I know you've had a few rough years, but I've had my fair share of tragedy too. I know what it's like to worry.
I've been locked up, buried alive, thrown in rivers, and I nearly took a two-week trip to Siberia in the back of a prison van.
By comparison, this injury I have is nothing to worry about.
Let me tell you a story about when I was really worried—the test of the *Mirror* handcuffs.

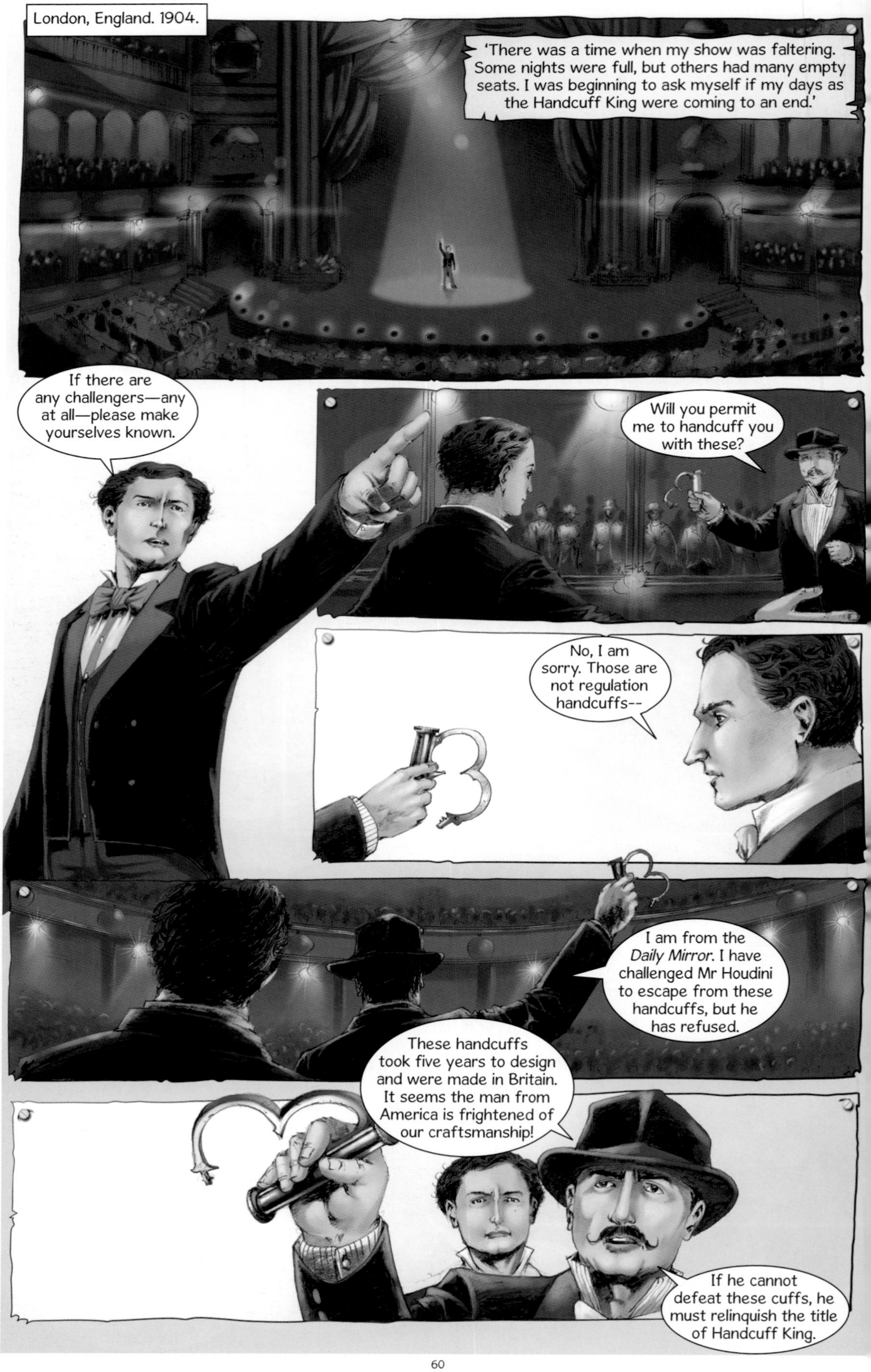
London, England. 1904.
'There was a time when my show was faltering. Some nights were full, but others had many empty seats. I was beginning to ask myself if my days as the Handcuff King were coming to an end.'
If there are any challengers—any at all—please make yourselves known.
Will you permit me to handcuff you with these?
No, I am sorry. Those are not regulation handcuffs--
I am from the *Daily Mirror*. I have challenged Mr Houdini to escape from these handcuffs, but he has refused.
These handcuffs took five years to design and were made in Britain. It seems the man from America is frightened of our craftsmanship!
If he cannot defeat these cuffs, he must relinquish the title of Handcuff King.

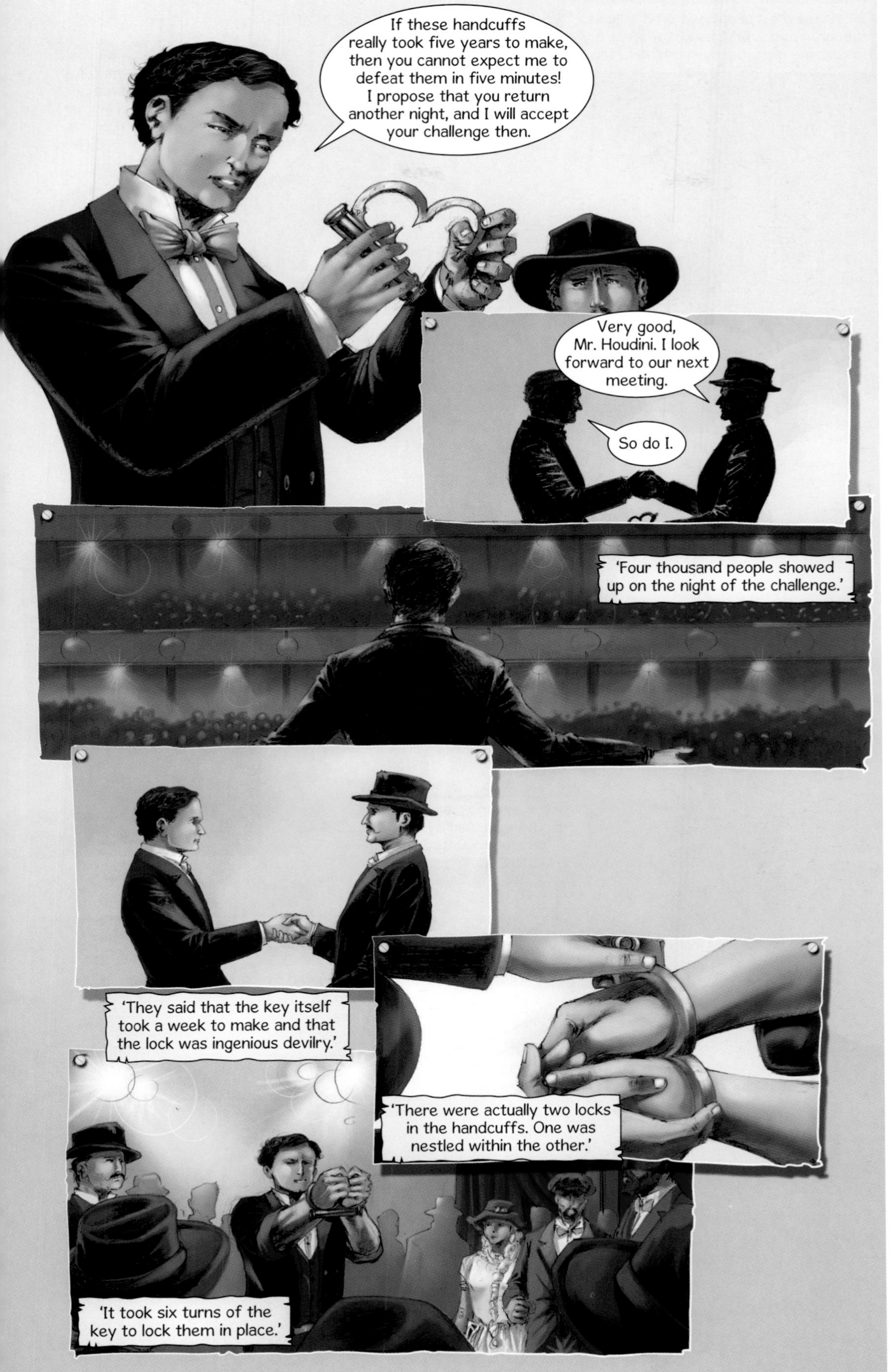
If these handcuffs really took five years to make, then you cannot expect me to defeat them in five minutes! I propose that you return another night, and I will accept your challenge then.
Very good, Mr. Houdini. I look forward to our next meeting.
So do I.
'Four thousand people showed up on the night of the challenge.'
'They said that the key itself took a week to make and that the lock was ingenious devilry.'
'There were actually two locks in the handcuffs. One was nestled within the other.'
'It took six turns of the key to lock them in place.'

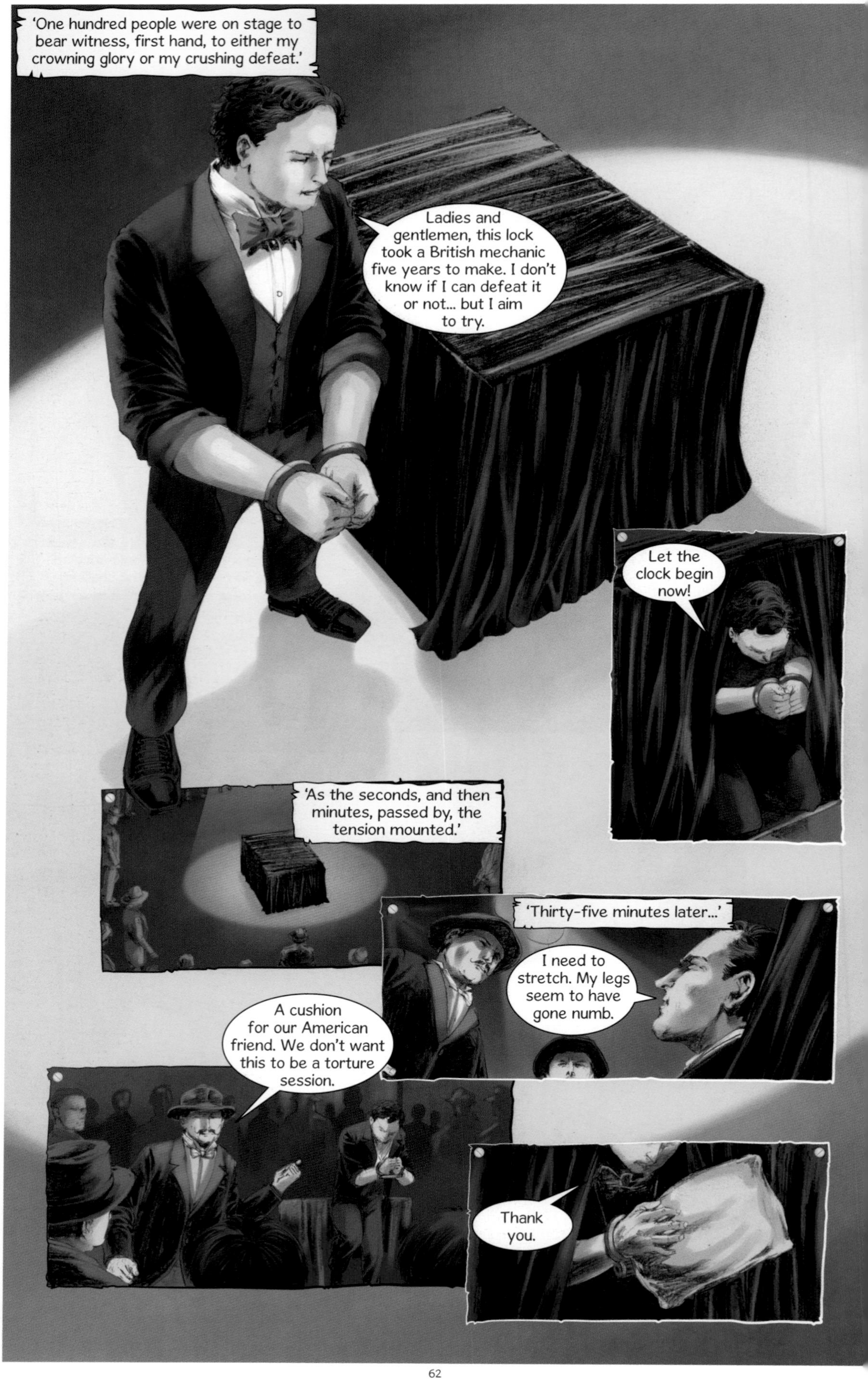
'One hundred people were on stage to bear witness, first hand, to either my crowning glory or my crushing defeat.'
Ladies and gentlemen, this lock took a British mechanic five years to make. I don't know if I can defeat it or not... but I aim to try.
Let the clock begin now!
'As the seconds, and then minutes, passed by, the tension mounted.'
'Thirty-five minutes later...'
I need to stretch. My legs seem to have gone numb.
A cushion for our American friend. We don't want this to be a torture session.
Thank you.

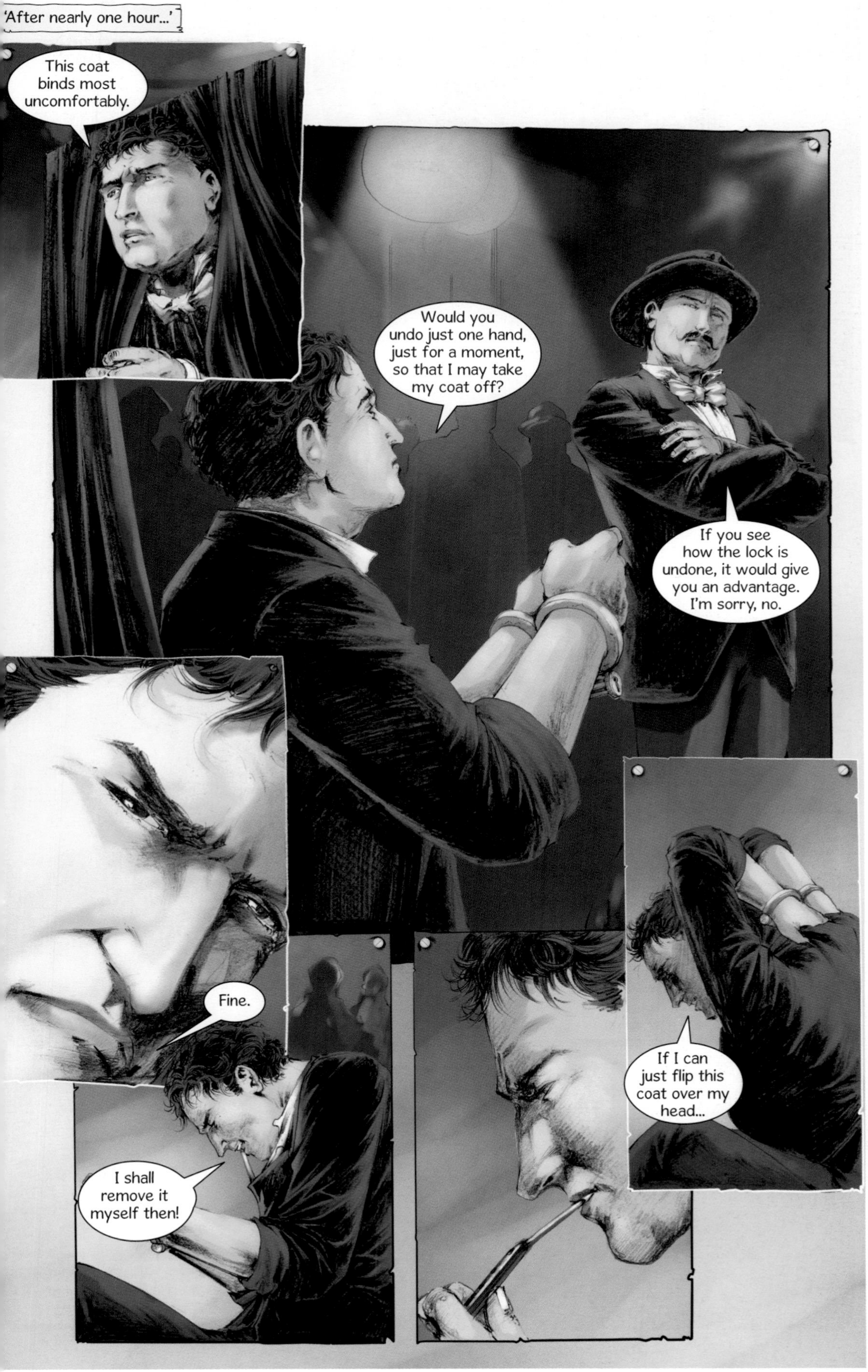
'After nearly one hour...'
This coat binds most uncomfortably.
Would you undo just one hand, just for a moment, so that I may take my coat off?
If you see how the lock is undone, it would give you an advantage. I'm sorry, no.
Fine.
I shall remove it myself then!
If I can just flip this coat over my head...

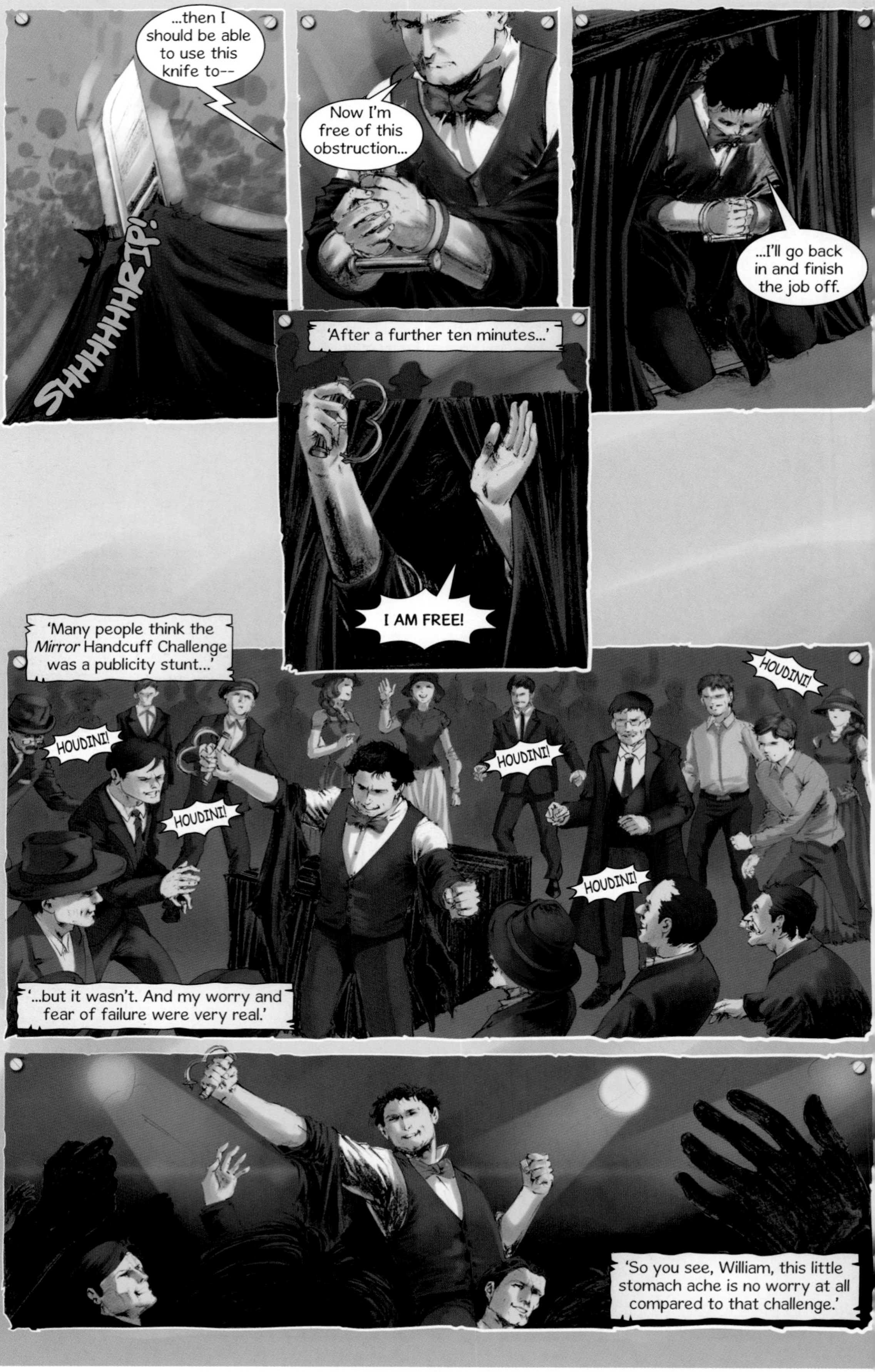
...then I should be able to use this knife to--
SHHHHHRIP!
Now I'm free of this obstruction...
...I'll go back in and finish the job off.
'After a further ten minutes...'
I AM FREE!
'Many people think the *Mirror* Handcuff Challenge was a publicity stunt...'
HOUDINI!
HOUDINI!
HOUDINI!
HOUDINI!
HOUDINI!
'...but it wasn't. And my worry and fear of failure were very real.'
'So you see, William, this little stomach ache is no worry at all compared to that challenge.'

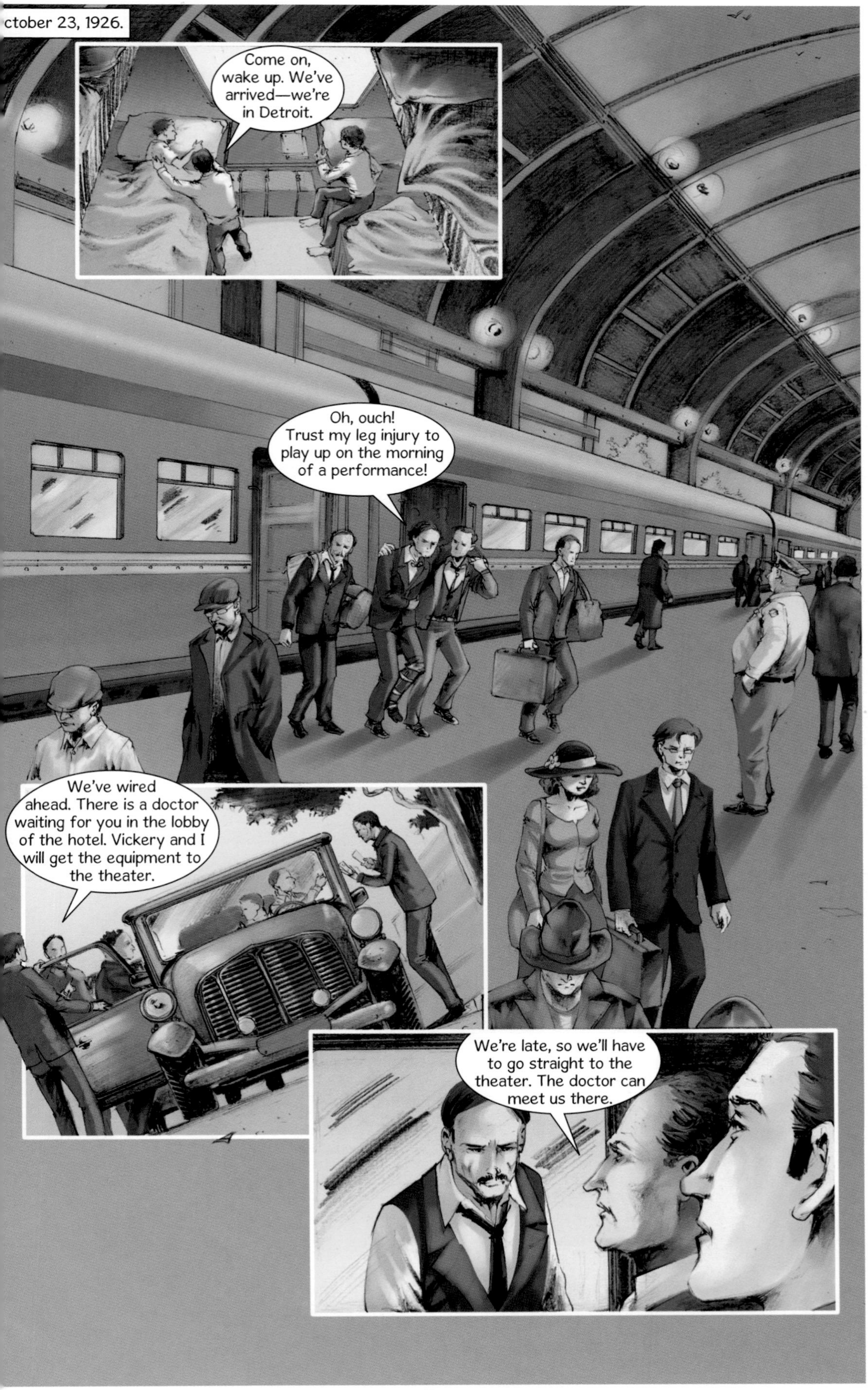
ctober 23, 1926.
Come on, wake up. We've arrived—we're in Detroit.
Oh, ouch! Trust my leg injury to play up on the morning of a performance!
We've wired ahead. There is a doctor waiting for you in the lobby of the hotel. Vickery and I will get the equipment to the theater.
We're late, so we'll have to go straight to the theater. The doctor can meet us there.

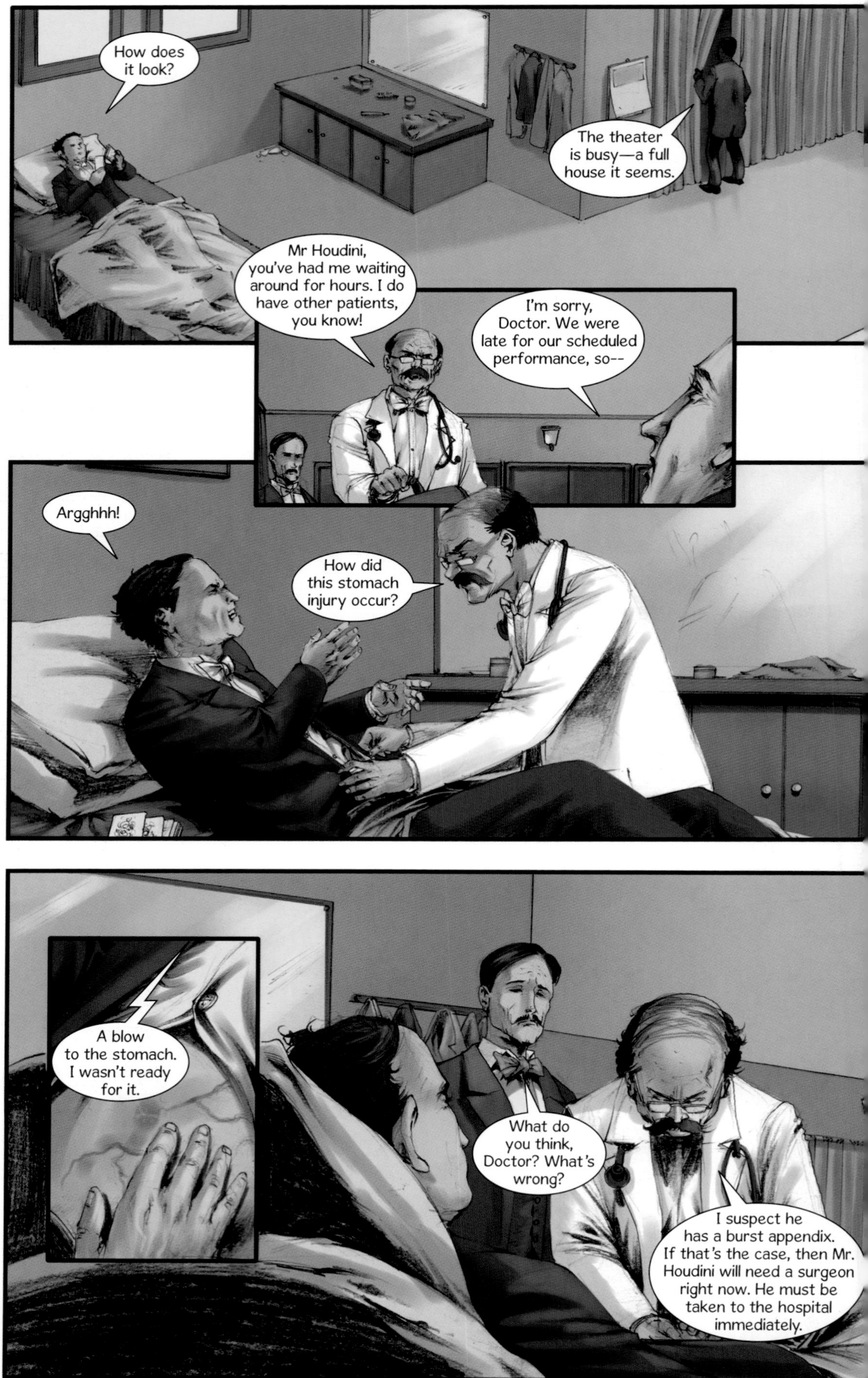
How does it look?
The theater is busy—a full house it seems.
Mr Houdini, you've had me waiting around for hours. I do have other patients, you know!
I'm sorry, Doctor. We were late for our scheduled performance, so--
Argghhh!
How did this stomach injury occur?
A blow to the stomach. I wasn't ready for it.
What do you think, Doctor? What's wrong?
I suspect he has a burst appendix. If that's the case, then Mr. Houdini will need a surgeon right now. He must be taken to the hospital immediately.

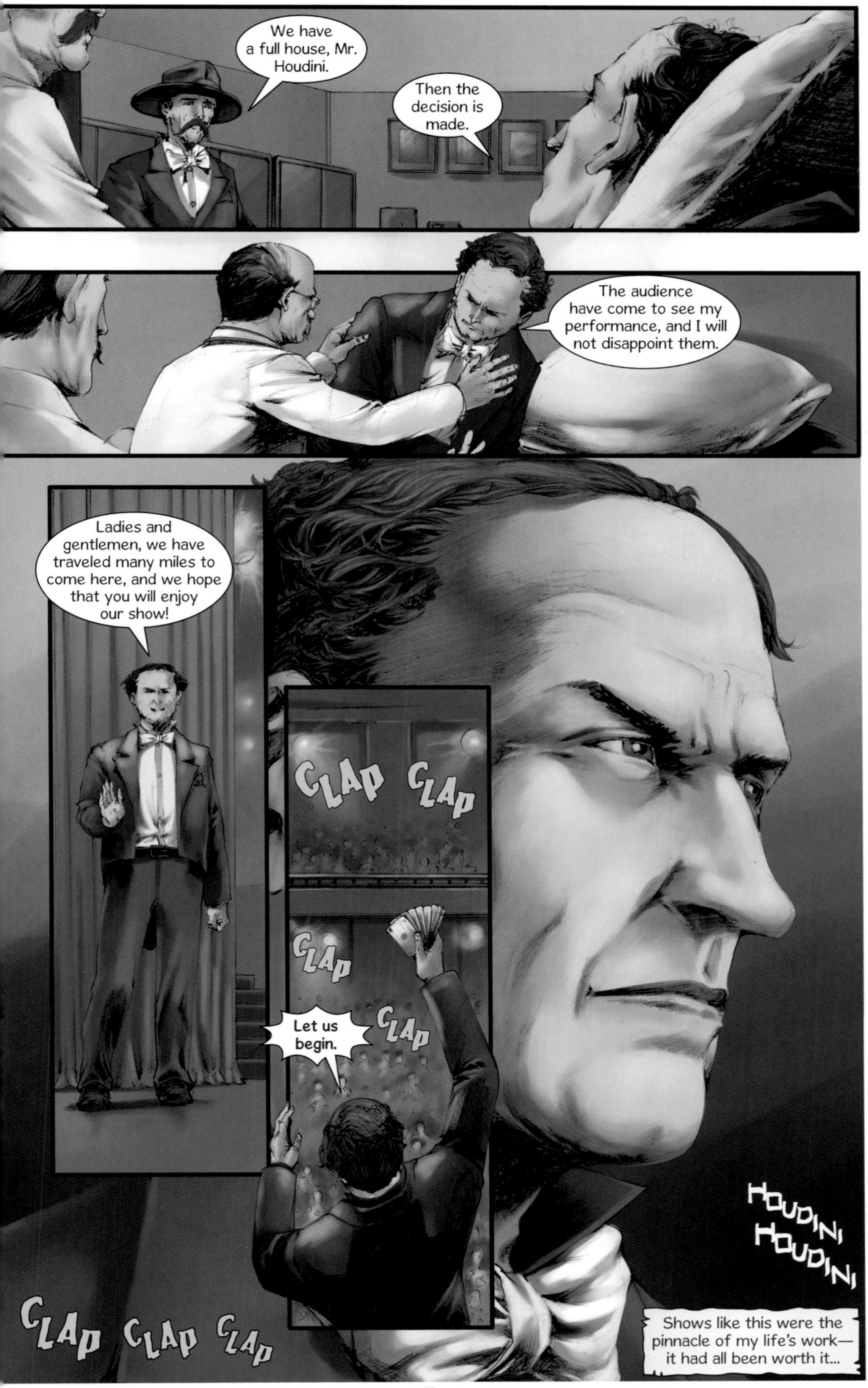
We have a full house, Mr. Houdini.
Then the decision is made.
The audience have come to see my performance, and I will not disappoint them.
Ladies and gentlemen, we have traveled many miles to come here, and we hope that you will enjoy our show!
CLAP CLAP
CLAP
Let us begin.
CLAP
CLAP CLAP CLAP
HOUDINI HOUDINI
Shows like this were the pinnacle of my life's work—it had all been worth it...

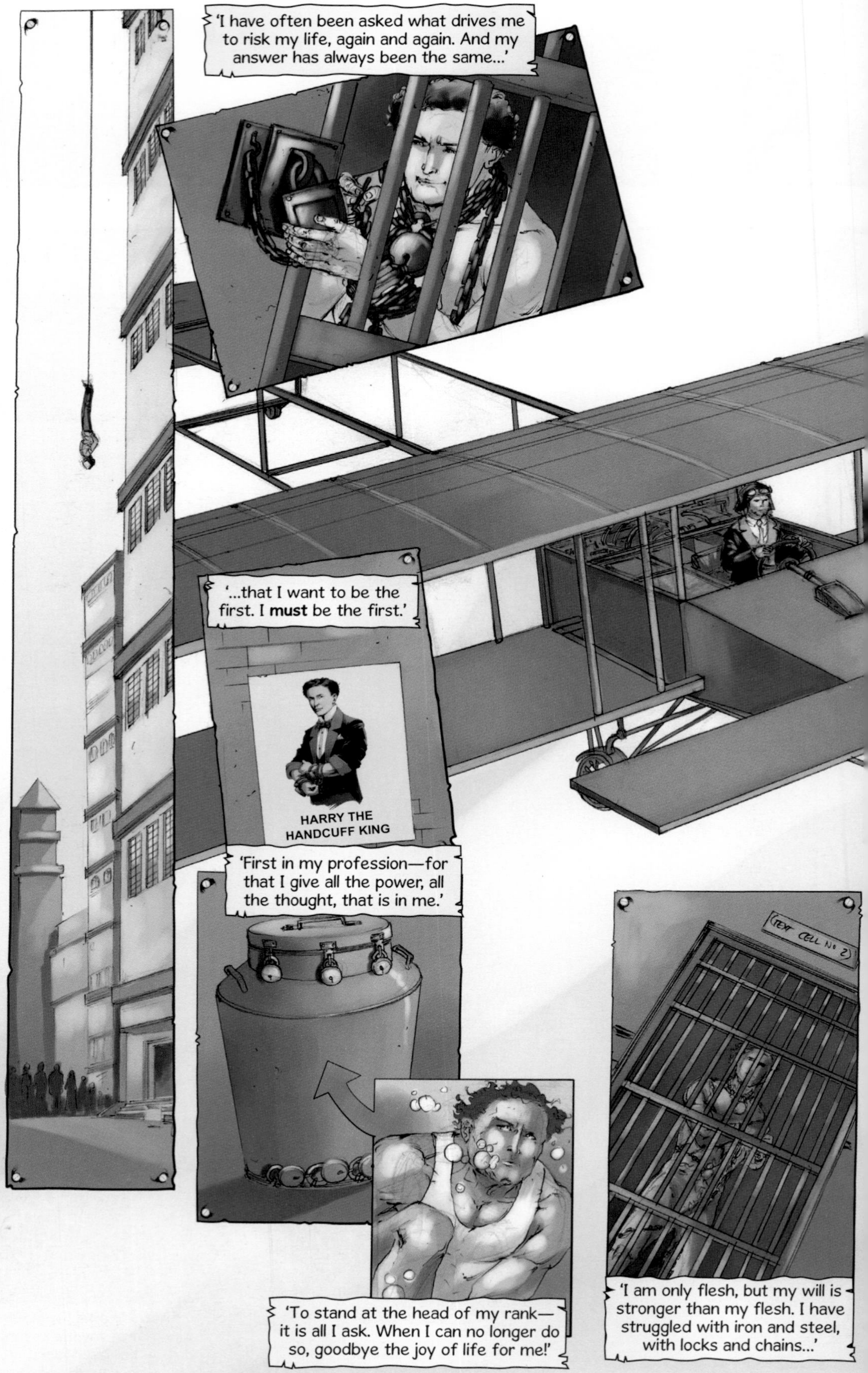
'I have often been asked what drives me to risk my life, again and again. And my answer has always been the same...'
'...that I want to be the first. I **must** be the first.'
HARRY THE HANDCUFF KING
'First in my profession—for that I give all the power, all the thought, that is in me.'
(TEXT CELL No 2)
'To stand at the head of my rank—it is all I ask. When I can no longer do so, goodbye the joy of life for me!'
'I am only flesh, but my will is stronger than my flesh. I have struggled with iron and steel, with locks and chains...'

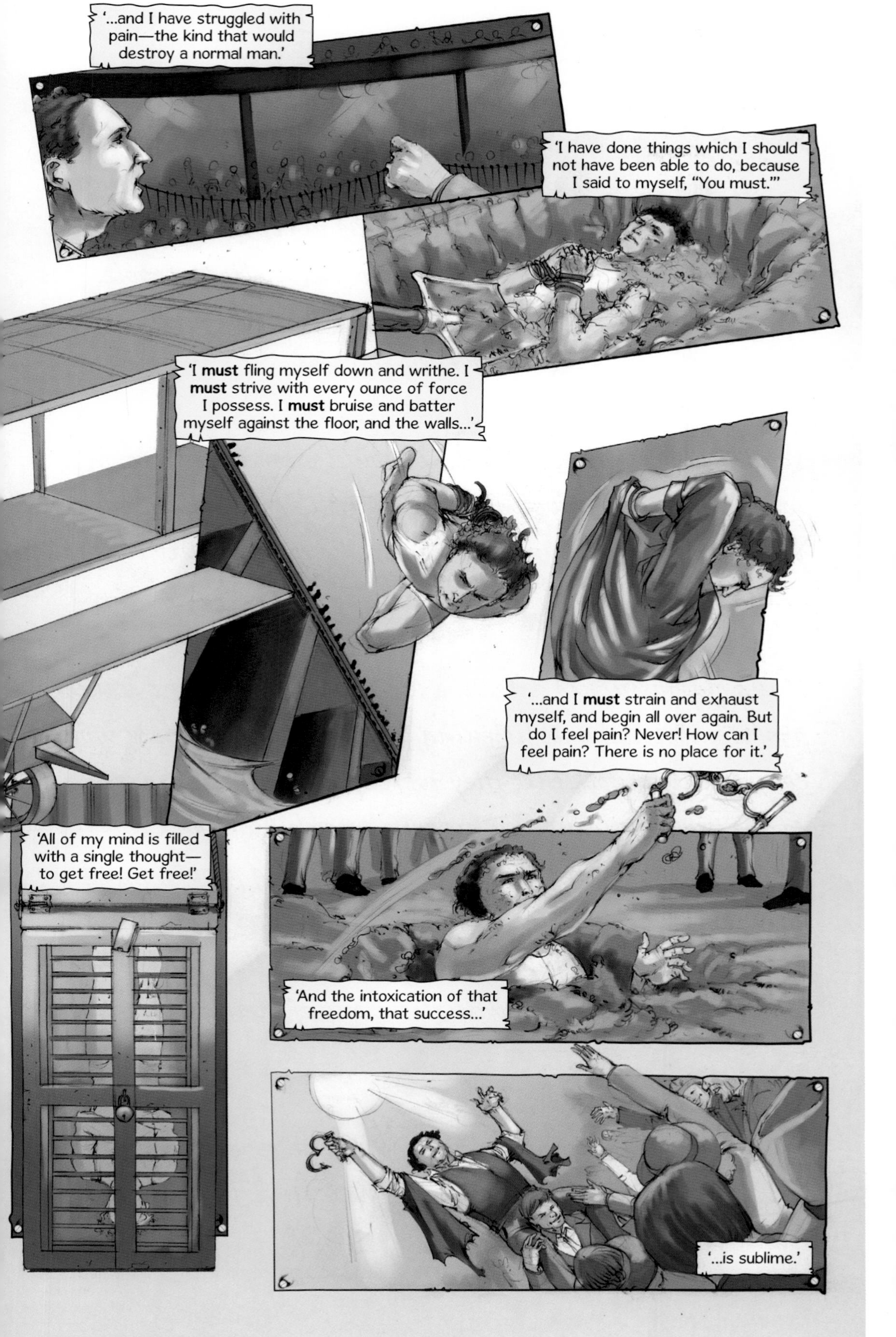
'...and I have struggled with pain—the kind that would destroy a normal man.'
'I have done things which I should not have been able to do, because I said to myself, "You must."'
'I **must** fling myself down and writhe. I **must** strive with every ounce of force I possess. I **must** bruise and batter myself against the floor, and the walls...'
'...and I **must** strain and exhaust myself, and begin all over again. But do I feel pain? Never! How can I feel pain? There is no place for it.'
'All of my mind is filled with a single thought—to get free! Get free!'
'And the intoxication of that freedom, that success...'
'...is sublime.'

October 24, 1926

I wonder if Houdini would be offended if I included in my book the fact that he and his wife used to lie to people. It is actually the truth and, if Houdini allows me, here is what I will write in my book:

Young Harry and Bess Houdini would often enter a town when they were traveling with Dr. Hill's Medicine Show and pretend to be mediums, claiming to have the ability to speak with the dead.

Using old-fashioned detective work, such as reading names from tombstones and listening to town gossip, the pair would convince townsfolk that they were speaking with the spirits. At the time, Houdini and his wife were hungry and desperate. However, they were still deceiving people, many of whom were seeking comfort from relatives lost long ago. Eventually, Houdini and his wife realized that they were doing wrong, and left spiritualism out of their act.

October 25, 1926

I have received a telegram from William reporting that Houdini is in hospital. Apparently he is suffering from a ruptured appendix.

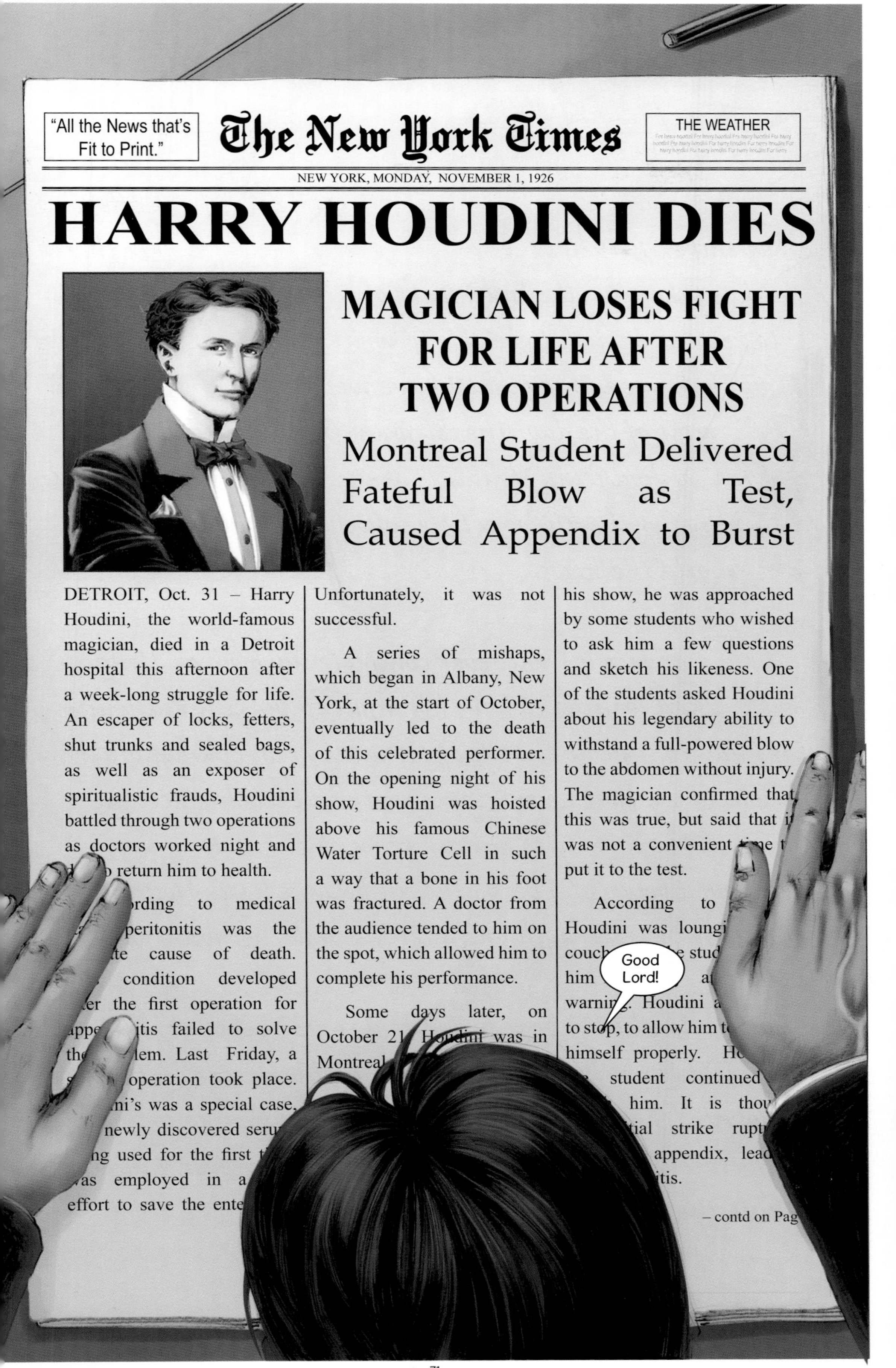

"All the News that's Fit to Print."

The New York Times

THE WEATHER

NEW YORK, MONDAY, NOVEMBER 1, 1926

# HARRY HOUDINI DIES

## MAGICIAN LOSES FIGHT FOR LIFE AFTER TWO OPERATIONS

### Montreal Student Delivered Fateful Blow as Test, Caused Appendix to Burst

DETROIT, Oct. 31 – Harry Houdini, the world-famous magician, died in a Detroit hospital this afternoon after a week-long struggle for life. An escaper of locks, fetters, shut trunks and sealed bags, as well as an exposer of spiritualistic frauds, Houdini battled through two operations as doctors worked night and d... return him to health.

...rding to medical ... peritonitis was the ...te cause of death. ... condition developed ...er the first operation for appe...itis failed to solve th...lem. Last Friday, a s... operation took place. ...ni's was a special case, ... newly discovered seru... ...ng used for the first t... ...as employed in a... effort to save the ente...

Unfortunately, it was not successful.

A series of mishaps, which began in Albany, New York, at the start of October, eventually led to the death of this celebrated performer. On the opening night of his show, Houdini was hoisted above his famous Chinese Water Torture Cell in such a way that a bone in his foot was fractured. A doctor from the audience tended to him on the spot, which allowed him to complete his performance.

Some days later, on October 21 ... was in Montrea...

his show, he was approached by some students who wished to ask him a few questions and sketch his likeness. One of the students asked Houdini about his legendary ability to withstand a full-powered blow to the abdomen without injury. The magician confirmed that this was true, but said that i... was not a convenient ... put it to the test.

According to ... Houdini was loungi... couch ... stud... him ... a... warnin... Houdini a... to stop, to allow him t... himself properly. H... ... student continued ... him. It is thou... ...tial strike rupt... ... appendix, lead... ...itis.

– contd on Pag...

Good Lord!

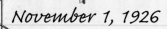

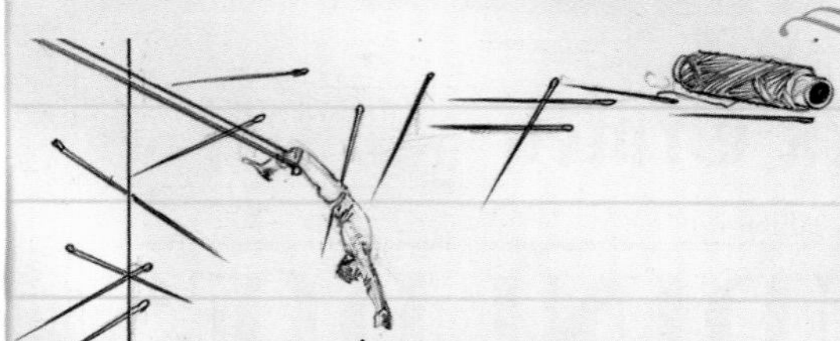

*November 1, 1926*

*It has taken me the better part of a day
to recover enough to be able to write. I am
not ashamed to say that I have wept for
most of the day. The telegram from William,
announcing Houdini's death, arrived soon
after the Times article which has told a shocked
world the news.*

*I am not sure if I will ever complete my book on Houdini
now. I had wanted to have his input to make it authentic.
If I had to sum up the life of Houdini in one paragraph,
I would say that he overcame every obstacle he faced in
life—from poverty to hunger, from obscurity to injury,
and even betrayal. Every time life became hard, Houdini
increased his strength and met his problems with force.*

*Harry Houdini gave so much to us—to me, personally; to
my nephew, William; and to the world. He was certainly
rewarded, and given the love and admiration he so
desperately craved. He will live among us forever. I do not
think the world will ever forget him.*

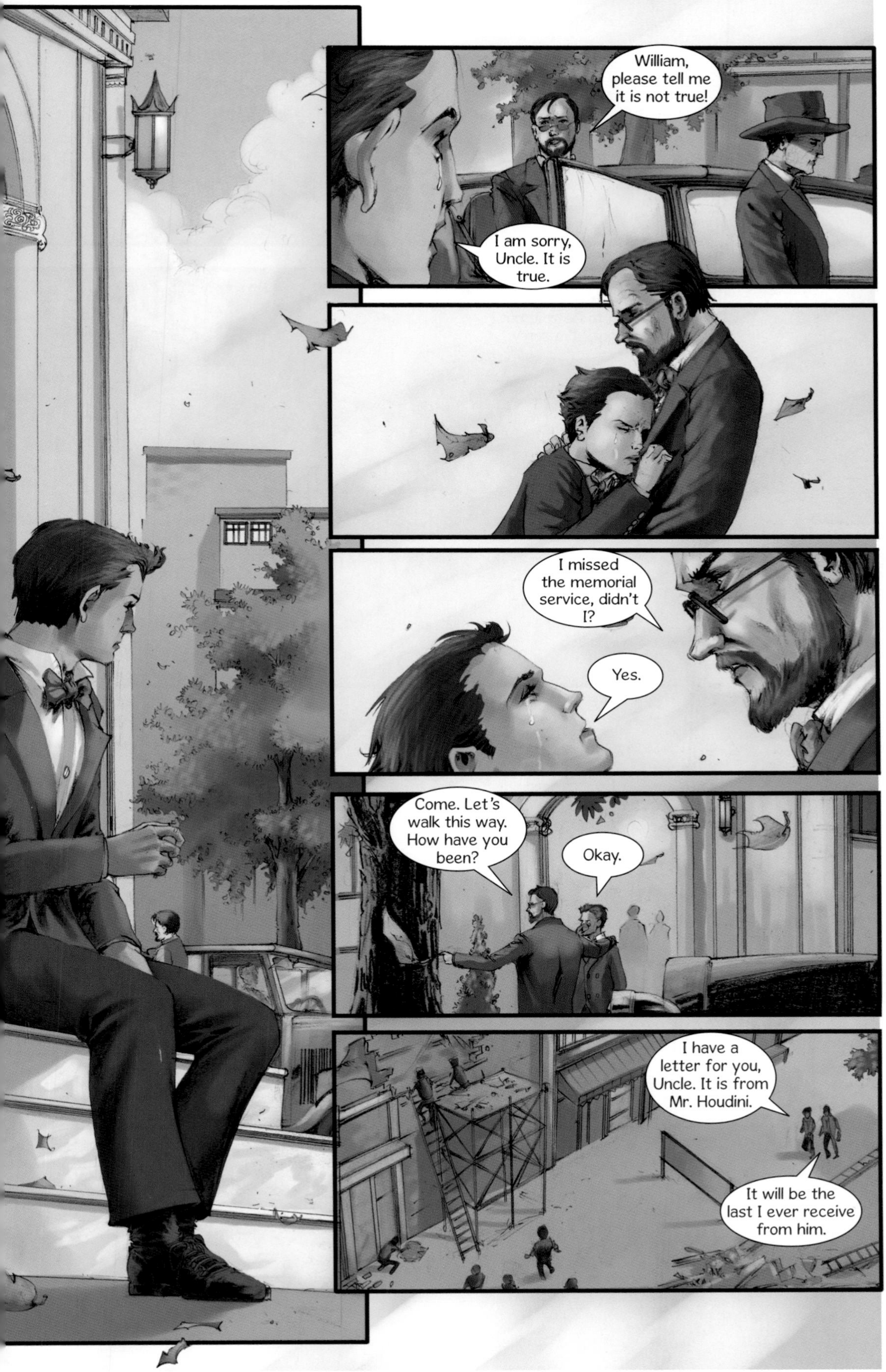
William, please tell me it is not true!
I am sorry, Uncle. It is true.
I missed the memorial service, didn't I?
Yes.
Come. Let's walk this way. How have you been?
Okay.
I have a letter for you, Uncle. It is from Mr. Houdini.
It will be the last I ever receive from him.

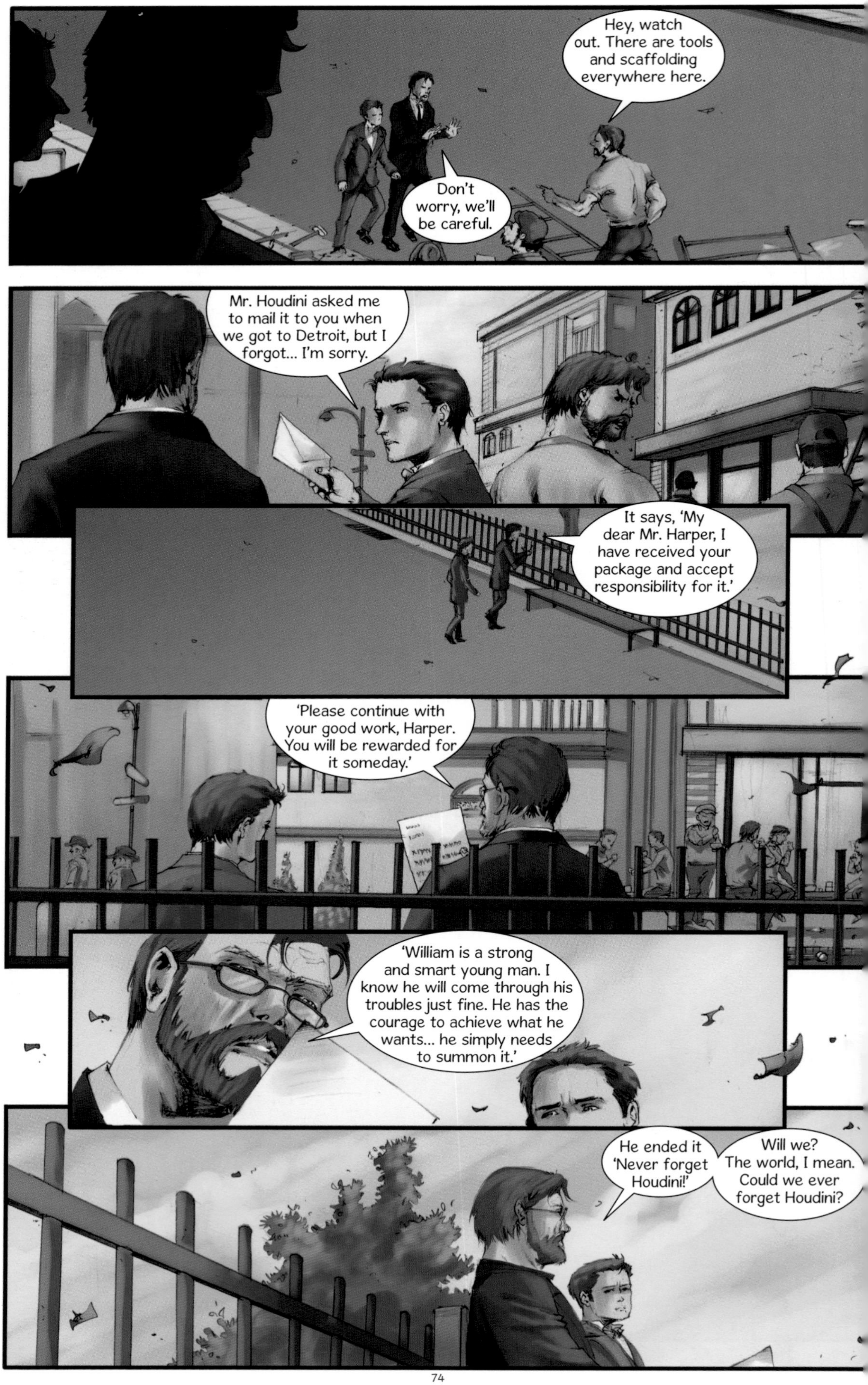

Hey, watch out. There are tools and scaffolding everywhere here.
Don't worry, we'll be careful.
Mr. Houdini asked me to mail it to you when we got to Detroit, but I forgot... I'm sorry.
It says, 'My dear Mr. Harper, I have received your package and accept responsibility for it.'
'Please continue with your good work, Harper. You will be rewarded for it someday.'
'William is a strong and smart young man. I know he will come through his troubles just fine. He has the courage to achieve what he wants... he simply needs to summon it.'
He ended it 'Never forget Houdini!'
Will we? The world, I mean. Could we ever forget Houdini?

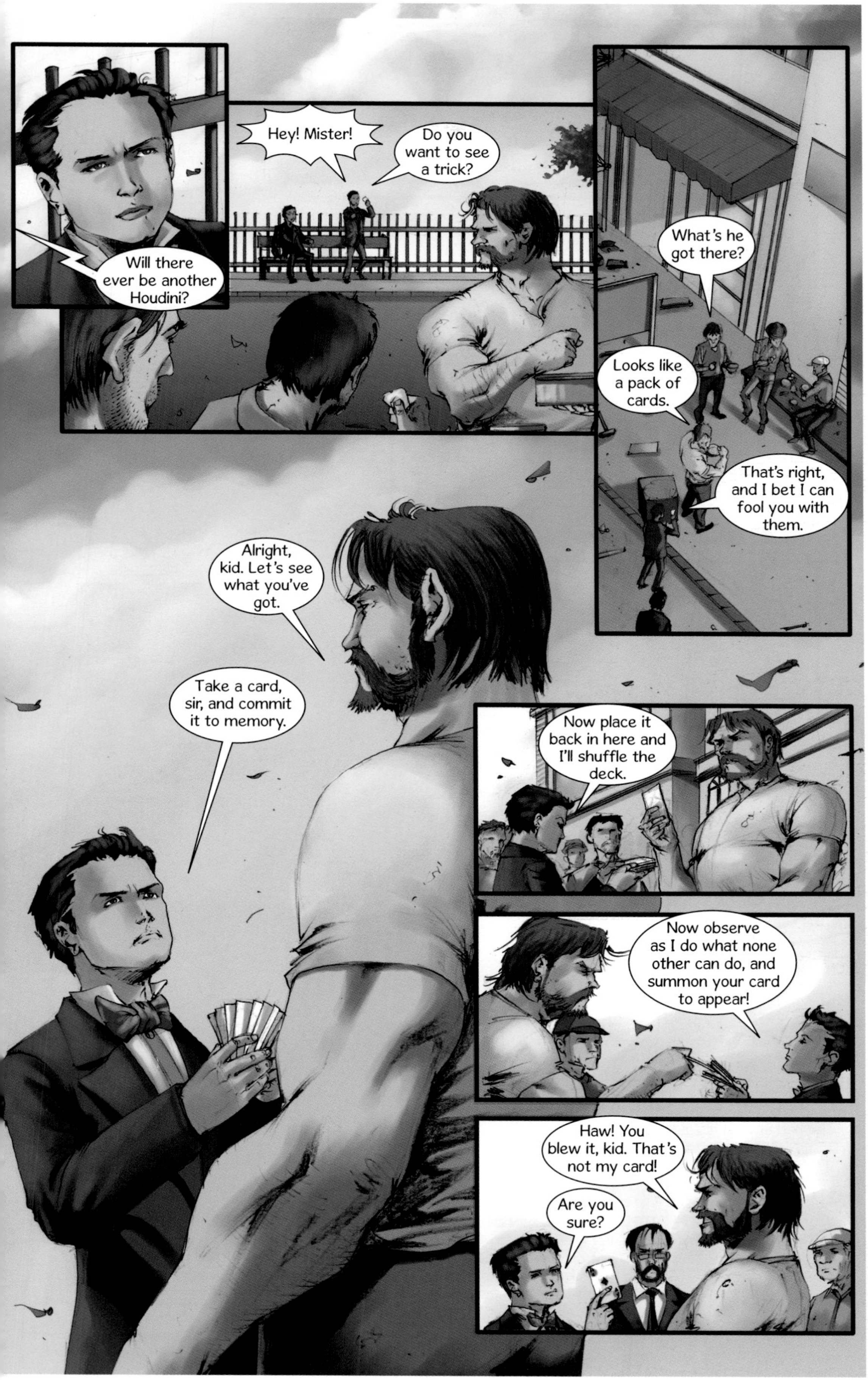
Will there ever be another Houdini?
Hey! Mister!
Do you want to see a trick?
What's he got there?
Looks like a pack of cards.
That's right, and I bet I can fool you with them.
Alright, kid. Let's see what you've got.
Take a card, sir, and commit it to memory.
Now place it back in here and I'll shuffle the deck.
Now observe as I do what none other can do, and summon your card to appear!
Haw! You blew it, kid. That's not my card!
Are you sure?

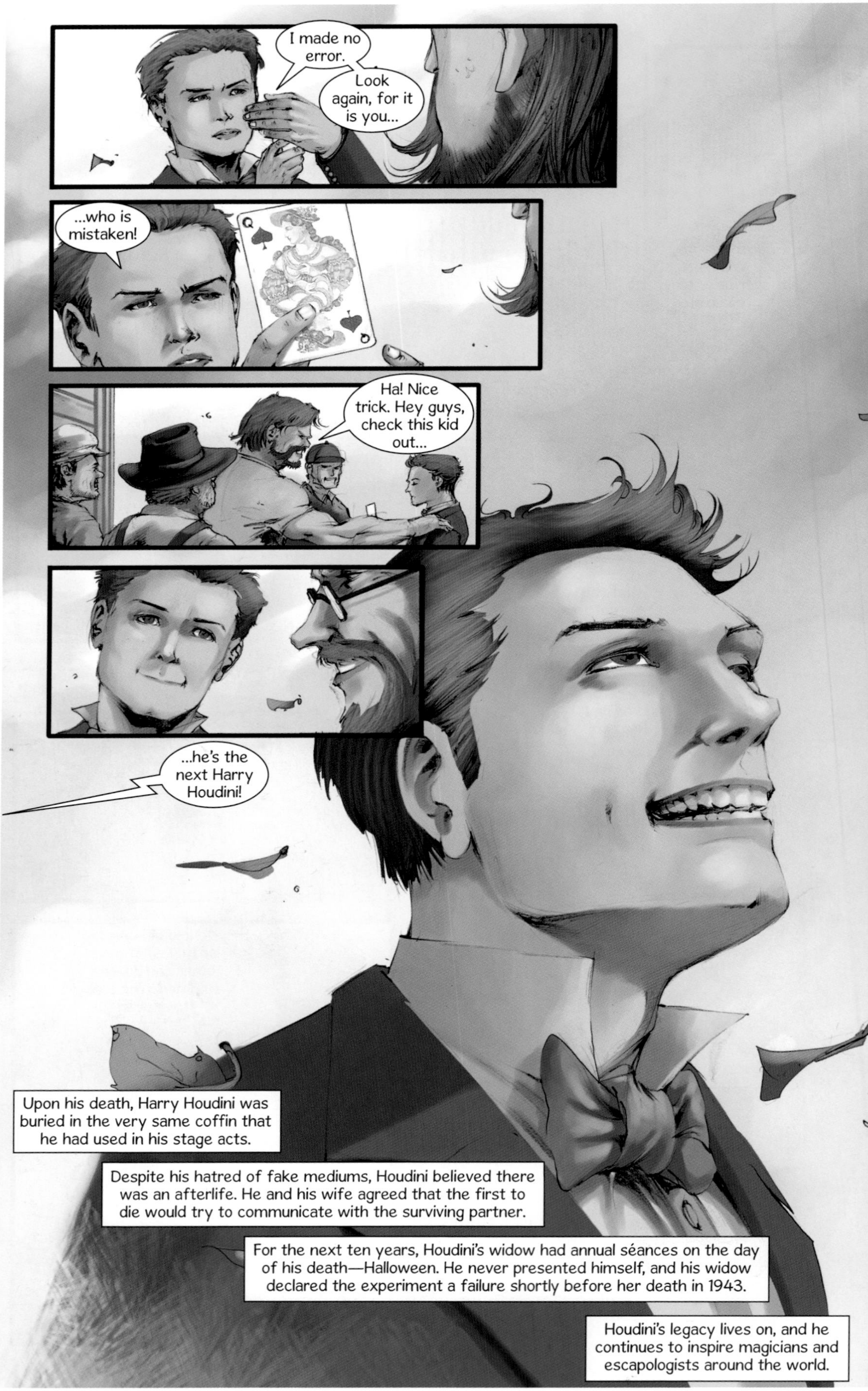
I made no error.
Look again, for it is you...
...who is mistaken!
Ha! Nice trick. Hey guys, check this kid out...
...he's the next Harry Houdini!
Upon his death, Harry Houdini was buried in the very same coffin that he had used in his stage acts.
Despite his hatred of fake mediums, Houdini believed there was an afterlife. He and his wife agreed that the first to die would try to communicate with the surviving partner.
For the next ten years, Houdini's widow had annual séances on the day of his death—Halloween. He never presented himself, and his widow declared the experiment a failure shortly before her death in 1943.
Houdini's legacy lives on, and he continues to inspire magicians and escapologists around the world.

**CAMPFIRE**™

## About Us

It is nighttime in the forest. The sky is black, studded with countless stars. A campfire is crackling, and the storytelling has begun—stories about love and wisdom, conflict and power, dreams and identity, courage and adventure, survival against all odds, and hope against all hope. In the warm, cheerful radiance of the campfire, the storyteller's audience is captivated, as in a trance. Even the trees and the earth and the animals of the forest seem to have fallen silent, bewitched.

Inspired by this enduring relationship between a campfire and gripping storytelling, we bring you four series of *Campfire Graphic Novels*:

Our *Classic* tales adapt timeless literature from some of the greatest writers ever.

Our *Mythology* series features epics, myths and legends from around the world, tales that transport readers to lands of mystery and magic.

Our *Biography* titles bring to life remarkable and inspiring figures from history.

Our *Original* line showcases brand new characters and stories from some of today's most talented graphic novelists and illustrators.

We hope you will gather around our campfire and discover the fascinating stories and characters inside our books.

# THE WORLD OF MAGIC

## FAMOUS MAGIC TRICKS EXPOSED!

### SAWING A LADY IN HALF

This is a very popular magic trick, which involves creating the illusion of sawing a woman's body in half. The woman lies in a box, which is placed on a table, and the magician passes a blade through her. The body is 'cut' in two and the 'pieces' are moved apart!

**HOW IS IT DONE?**

- The front of the box faces the audience, to make it look like the woman is placed in the path of the saw. However, the box is deeper than it seems (not visible to the audience), and the woman curls up her legs so that the blade does not touch her.

- The feet the audience see are simply fake ones which are operated with an electric motor! They replace the woman's feet as she curls up her legs.

### DID YOU KNOW?

★ The world's most dangerous trick is believed to be the Bullet Catch where a bullet is fired directly at the performer, and he catches it between his teeth. It is believed that at least 15 magicians have lost their lives while performing this trick!

### THE BALDUCCI LEVITATION

Have you ever seen David Blaine, the famous street performer, raise himself off the ground? This trick is called the Balducci Levitation in which the performer's feet appear to lift off the ground by a few inches. A short act that does not usually last for more than five seconds, it ends with the performer's feet landing back on solid ground.

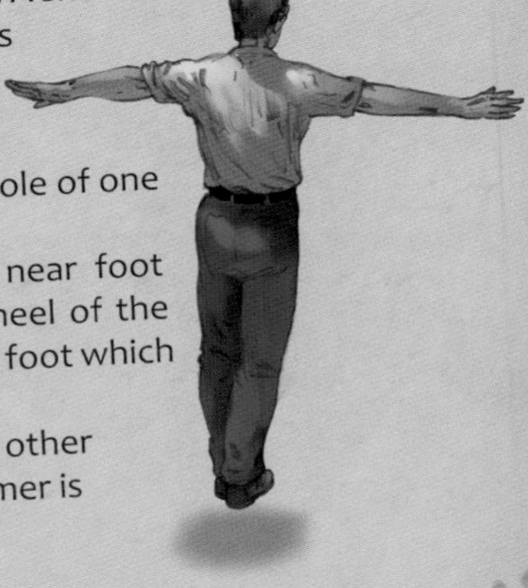

**HOW IS IT DONE?**

- The performer stands so that the audience can see the whole of one foot, but only the heel of the other.

- Keeping both ankles together, the performer lifts the near foot (visible to the audience) off the ground, as well as the heel of the other foot. The body's weight then rests on the toes of the foot which are hidden from the view of the audience.

- The audience see the whole of one foot and the heel of the other lifting off the ground, creating the illusion that the performer is hovering in mid-air.

# THE INDIAN ROPE TRICK

This mysterious trick was believed to have been performed by magicians of the East, centuries ago. First, the magician hurls a rope into the air. It stands erect and the magician's assistant disappears up it, and refuses to return. The magician then follows him up the rope and the sounds of a fight are heard. Suddenly, the dismembered limbs of the assistant fall to the ground. The magician climbs down, puts the parts in a basket and covers it with a cloth. And hey presto! The assistant springs out of the basket in one piece!

## HOW IS IT DONE?

This trick was usually performed at night between two trees or similar objects. A strong wire was tied high up between the trees and was not visible to the spectators. The rope, which had a wooden ball at its top, got hooked to the wire as it was thrown up. The assistant would climb up easily, secure the rope to the wire and then the magician would follow him. The strong wire would support the weight of the two men. Simple enough. But what about the body parts? They were parts of a dead monkey dressed in clothes similar to the assistant's! And the last bit of the act: the 'intact' boy would leap out from under the magician's large coat where he was hidden!

# MAGNETIC MATCHES

This is a simple trick you can try yourself. Firstly, the magician claims that he has the power to make matchsticks magnetic. He then slides a matchbox open a quarter of the way to prove that it is an ordinary box of matches. He puts it on a table, passes his hand over it and chants a few magic words. Then he opens the box upside down, holding it by the sides with his fingers. Amazingly, none of the sticks fall out. The magician then waves his hand over the box again and all the matches fall out as he 'de-magnetizes' them!

## HOW IS IT DONE?

- A box of matches is opened. A single matchstick is taken out and cut to the size of the width of the box. It is placed across the other sticks, at the box's halfway point. It should be pressed in so that it holds the other sticks in place, and also allows the box to be opened and closed easily. This ensures the sticks can't fall out when the box is overturned. A slight pressing of the sides of the box loosens the stick holding the rest in place, and they all fall out. Simple, isn't it?

## DID YOU KNOW?

★ Charles Dickens, the great 19th-century novelist, was an amateur magician!

★ Prince Charles, the prince of Wales, has a keen interest in illusionism and is a member of *The Magic Circle*—an organization committed to magic!